Adult Entertainment

Chloe Poems

route

Chloe Poems

Chloe Poems could be Robin Hood, if you lose the Lincoln Green and re-cover him with gingham. Their redistribution policy is pretty much the same and they both love their merry men. Chloe Poems could be Big Red Riding Hood, skipping through the woods, chased by the wolf but never fooled by grandmother's big eyes and teeth. Either way, one thing is for sure, Chloe Poems is a hood.

First Published in 2002 by Route
School Lane, Glasshoughton, West Yorks, WF10 4QH
e-mail: books@route-online.com

ISBN: 1 901927 18 0

Cover Design: Andy Campbell
Cover Images: Kevin Reynolds

Support
Ian Daley, Roisin Heycock, Liz O'Neil, Dean Smith

Printed by Bookmarque Ltd, Croydon, Surrey

CD Recorded live at Milo, Leeds 21 May 2002
CD recorded and duplicated by Clipstore, Leeds
Recording Engineer: Geoff Glout
Mastering Engineer: Warwick Pilmer

A catalogue for this book is available from the British Library

Full details of the Route programme of books
can be found on our website
www.route-online.com

Route is the fiction imprint of YAC, a registered charity No 1007443

YAC is supported by
Yorkshire Arts, Wakefield MDC, West Yorkshire Grants

To Susan and Pearl -
the pals of my halcyon days
Cheers burds
Oh, and, er, Robbie and Gary -
To good times, past, present and future

Contents

FOREWORD by Gary McMahon

Lights down, trippy music fades and cabaret tables ripple in the dark because something more than an act is stepping into the spotlight, dressed like a clown in a friary.

'O-my-god,' looking like she's shuffled off the street into *Sweet Charity*, her wide-eyed sense of wonder wonders *Why me?* but life's so wild and weird, so camp and kinky, (*they'd never believe it*) so *WwOw!why not? Let's wing it!* He's had this same experience backwards, finishing a tour and finding himself on the street. After all, 'It's a world: things happen.'

Ladies and gentlemen, all the way from Liverpool, via Gallifrey, gingham diva, radical agenda bender, agony aunt and great aunty establishment, Chloe Poems.

Who? 'Alright! AAALLLRRRIGHT! I'm a gay-socialist-transvestite-poet,' and that's as close to compromise as she gets.

Weaving homespun philosophy into a technicolor gingham gown, gleefully courting controversy and tackling the hecklers, making a community out of an audience, this profound egoist and selfless vessel will encourage you to be the best that you can be, as he puts his art on the line to create a space where theatre can push the boundaries and fuck the consequences. Chloe is doing for gingham what another Avenger did hell for leather. Spinning a metaphor on the run on the mic, on the page, his 'n' hers: fancy footwork in training shoes that dance around a paradox and shadow-box your expectations in free verse.

So obviously male and so clearly feminine, so clowning and furious, flippant and passionate, holy and sacrilegious, childlike yet canny from many lives past. An archetypal heritage of Shakespearean foolery and Rabelaisian carnival and Liverpudlian waggery is woven into her gingham tapestry. Listen:

'I love you all. I may not *like* you all. We may not be compatible. We may…sleep separately. But that's alright, because I love you all, and so I give you, all, Anal Energy.' Some tables look bemused about that, but it's free love in the gingham grand design, where no one is significant unless everybody is, all are needed to make this equilateral pattern, made iconic by a simple stroke of genius. The bard sends gingham love to you all, just so long as you understand that Society Is Evil and certain Very

9

Important Persons must die. He hopes that isn't too contradictory, but, well, there it is, and then again, 'I've said too much.'

Spontaneity is the first sign that the gingham diva is a living character, with the contradictions of a living character. After all, 'Give someone nerve-endings, love, and he's going to respond!' *My god*, palms aloft, *well don't you see?* Chloe's unpredictable appearances and blasphemous poetry make frisky headlines —

> **Scandal! 'The Queen Sucks Nazi Cock!'**
> **the police are called on behalf of Queen Elizabeth II to a**
> **street performance where a gingham getaway is one block**
> **ahead of the Tower…**

> **at the Edinburgh Fringe Festival, machismo climbs**
> **on-stage to get the radical tranny…**

> **at Quentin Crisp's funeral,**
> **a gathering of mourners at someone else's grave**
> **forgets how to cry**
> **at a vision of the diva in full gingham glory,**
> **'A *faux pas*! have I gone too far?'**

Improvising her kinky way out of a tight cliché, spontaneity is the mark of an artist in residence. Accident is the genesis of creativity, Patrick Troughton tells us, and ingenious accidents happen in these pages.

In the melancholy of a lost cause and the disillusion of a broken nation, in the restoration of idealism, with revolutionary naiveté and euphoric revelations of Spiritual Socialism, Chloe's outré poetry is coming out. And so many passageways — sex, drugs and dominoes, to name three — you're sure to find your own way in.

My access to Chloe's verse and way of being is through camp, camp as performance, yes, and camp as a flamboyant style of writing. Camp and Chloe: an operatic range as dynamic as punk and deft as ballet, with art nouveau flourishes and an urbane flair for irony — 'A leafing legacy of vines / You're now more inclined to call laughter lines' — whose teasing sense of timing cuts like Dorothy Parker's finger nails, or eases the tensions of a nation.

Like 'Stupid Intellectual', many anally retentive academics, in no position to receive Anal Energy, and in no mood for literary hijinks, though camper than Batman on campus in mortar board and gown, will chastise, edit and dismiss as redundant any such camp and its indulgent extravagance. They want to spank Chloe's bottom. Can I have a word with you about that?

Camp is so misunderstood that any artist donning its guise faces a gruelling battle for recognition. Camp is misconstrued as insincere because it highlights distance between performance and existence. The distance is the focal length of a mirror. It's an ironic distance, with subversive implications for self-awareness: who do you think you are?

Camp is a paradox, just like Chloe Poems. By overplaying a line, a role, a situation, yet remaining ironically and whimsically aloof, camp uses theatricality to show the artifice of the human condition and intimate the Bigger Picture. Bigger, even, than socialism. Aloof, like a witnessing consciousness, camp plays with observations made down the ages from Zen through Shakespeare to transactional analysis that all the world's a stage and all the men and women merely players. It makes a social construct of gender, so camp is sometimes transvestite, too.

Masculine-feminine is one topical polarity transcended by camp, but you'll find others here. Chloe's mischievous eloquence teases tensions between creation and destruction, right and wrong, gay and straight…at his best, moving between subjectivity and the Eye of God to show the Bigger Picture. Bigger, even, than socialism, but, in a society prostituted by commercialism and sucked off by celebrity and shafted by injustice, socialism will do.

So yes, *Why me?* Chloe suddenly steps off-stage to sit with her audience and complete the gingham pattern, leaving a hole in the show: we are all left looking at an empty spotlight, and some of the punters are getting restless. Over his shoulder, 'You see, it doesn't work, does it?' Alright. But let's remember, comrades, it doesn't work without *you*, too. And that's how she, Chloe, a character like you and I, just like the author himself, makes a community out of an audience. It's the wisdom of the clown. Camp makes social constructs of us all.

The first camp writer I ever read was William Shakespeare. He's dead now, but he was dripping with ironic affectation, exuberant metaphors and showboating rhetoric, clowns and transvestites teasing a paradox in panto and melodrama, yes, and a Third Eye looking over everybody's shoulder. With a life in theatre as actor, director, playwright and poet, pausing only to become a prostitute, Chloe Poems too conceives wordplay as performance.

Breathtaking rhythms and registers rise and fall on CD with this spellbound publication, from rhetorical tirade to intimate *tête-à-tête*. The CD bridges poetry from *Adult Entertainment* to *Universal Rentboy*, Chloe's first collection. It's a compelling delivery driven by outrage and *joi de vivre*, and, eavesdropping every stanza, a witnessing consciousness, looking over your shoulder as you read.

Chloe stitches the battle rents in her gingham flag under a lampshade and waits for a deadbeat society and the glittering literati to catch up. Camp style is ready to give the written word the infusion of energy and consciousness that changed popular music in the 20th century. This book, this clown, this artist, does all that.

Introduction

Hello comrades, and welcome to this, my second collection of lovely poetry - *Adult Entertainment*.

I was in such a befuddle about what to write for an introduction, and so turned to Betty, my trusted colleague and equal, and said 'Betty, my trusted colleague and equal, I'm in such a befuddle about what to write for this introduction, what do I do?' Betty quickly, succinctly, without even opening her mouth, said 'Just write what you believe in.' So I said 'Okay, that's a very good idea.'

I believe in Betty.

Also I believe intellect without instinct is akin to having the finest pedigree dog without a sense of smell, for no matter how well turned out it is, or how many tricks it's been taught, it's only half a dog if it can't sniff out, and therefore understand, the very many different types of shit. I believe some, not all, intellectuals, are only half an animal.

I don't believe that the children are our future, because we are not teaching them well and they are leading the way in rabid consumerism. Understanding and redressing this is the greatest love of all.

I believe in drugs. I believe in being off your tits in a great club with great music. I believe some people shouldn't take cocaine.

I don't believe Halle Berry winning an Oscar is an open door for all American women of colour. I believe only a huge redistribution of wealth and a free National Health Service could go some way to achieving that. I believe show business is a cancer and riddled with disease. I believe in entertainment. I believe I am an adult.

I believe in good food. I believe in sex. I believe in the freedom to explore its many recipes. I believe in over-eating.

I believe Margaret Thatcher to be the ultimate personification of evil. I believe if she was a drag king she would dress as Tony Blair. I believe Tony Blair would see this as a compliment.

I believe everyone should have a garden.

I don't believe Stephen Gately was brave for being forced by a national newspaper to come out, or indeed that Victoria Beckham is clever. I can't understand the show-business gay mafia's weird desire to turn cowards into heroes and idiots into geniuses. I believe Peter Tatchell is God. I believed in The Divine David. I believe that out gay people working in the most difficult conditions are truly heroes. I believe in being gay. I believe being gay is a small yet deeply significant part of my sense of humanity. I don't believe in ghettos.

I believe the world is sick with greed. I believe it can be cured. I believe in the anti-capitalist demonstrators. I believe in having a big camp laugh.

I believe in Dr Who.

I believe George Bush to be six of the Seven Horses of the Apocalypse. I believe if George Bush were a drag queen he would dress as Cherie Blair. I believe Cherie Blair would see this as a compliment. I believe Tony Blair to be the Seventh My Little Pony of the Apocalypse. I believe in the Socialist Alliance.

I believe I am stupid. I believe I am clever. I believe in booze. I don't believe in the religious Victorian or corporate view of right and wrong. I believe graciousness is achieved through love, respect and understanding a person's needs. I believe I can and can't be gracious. I believe malicious gossip can seriously damage emotional health. I believe malicious gossiping isn't gracious. I believe, to my shame, I have maliciously gossiped. I believe if I've said I love you, I've meant it.

I believe Peter Mullan's characterisation of Joe in *My Name is Joe* is the finest screen performance by an actor I have ever witnessed. I believe Ken Loach is God.

I believe Monica Lewinsky is the spitting image of a young Priscilla Presley. I believe Bill Clinton has an Elvis complex. I believe if Bill Clinton were a drag queen he would dress as Priscilla Presley and rejoice in coming all over himself. I believe Priscilla Presley would be horrified by this.

I believe in my family. I believe there is still a working class. I believe in Easter Egg Chocolate.

I believe deliberately provocative titles can encourage people who would not ordinarily read poetry, to read.

I believe in Buffy the Vampire Slayer.

I believe to know yourself you have to tell the truth to yourself. I believe in talking to yourself. I believe in walking your talk. I believe I have a poetic licence to kill. I believe I don't always get it right. I believe I have the right to get it wrong. I believe art in all its forms is deliciously malleable and it is our duty to bend and journey with it.

I believe I am an 85% water carbon-based life form, with a series of awe-inspiring nerve endings. I believe you are too. I believe in me, and therefore, somehow, I must believe in you.

I wish you health, happiness, healing,

Comrade Poems

PS I believe the revolution will not be plagiarised (in this book).

The Effeminate

Never underestimate the effeminate child
He is wise and wild beyond his years
His tears embroider a tapestry of survival
They mark the arrival of his ever evolving
Ever loving identity.

The effeminate is a firebreather
With little boy's drag on
A water carrier carrying a pitcher
A flagon containing gallons
Of experience and reserve
A reservoir of pain
And joi de vivre.
If the effeminate is as bold as brass
Then he sure as hell will make it shine.
The effeminate embraces
And tastes the grapes of wrath
The sweetest wine,
Is always two steps ahead
While seeming to lag behind
And can suddenly scissor-kick into quickstep
The intricacies of his incisor mind
And leave you blinded and reminded.
Never underestimate the effeminate.

If he were a fish
He'd be a deep-sea anomaly
A paradoxical mix of viscousness and solidity
A shape-shifting mass of undulating validity
So with friends like this
Who needs anemones?

The effeminate exists on many levels
He's more than at home with the angels and devils
Of his ever complex ideology
He is genius and idiot spasmodically.

The effeminate walks alone.

The effeminate in isolation
Is a potboiler of creation
But seemingly an irritation
To his friends and family.
He is a bastard child
Wandering lonely through a sea of parents
A misfit orbiting the outer sphere
But it's the safest place to wander
It's where you can't hear your father or mother call you queer.
You're just not quite right
Never your father's son
Nor mother's pride.
I imagine that's why some effeminates find themselves
Contemplating or even committing suicide.
These are dark places
Without glitter
Where the bitter and unjust meet and joust for supremacy.
It is necromancy of thought
Which plagues and ages,
It is the dog-eared pages
Of a book you never wanted to read
A desire you never wanted to need
The weed you never wanted to seed.
But the effeminate is more than a gardening analogy
More than a whimsical parody
Of sitcom inaccuracy
And vulgar interpretation.
He stands outrageously somewhere
Between form and inspiration.

He can be acetylene in his intensity
Ridiculous in his propensity
As he reclaims his wildest imaginings.
The effeminate can structure the most intricate ballet
Out of his silliest dillies and dallyings
A marrying of wit and movement
Something he would consider an improvement
On the real men surrounding.

Real men
Who denied him his courage
Real men
Who had the audacity to claim he was not like them
That he was flimsy dross, candyfloss, Diana Ross
Next to their hard-nosed granite and stone.
But the effeminate knows
Some real men also find it hard
To stand alone
Overbearingly hard
Especially in public toilets.
It's where real men have been known to understand
Even offer a helping hand
Where the hideous complexities
Of the once bullying playgrounds
Are left behind or quite simply overlooked.
Can you imagine the power the effeminate found
When he realised some real men
Just love to be fucked
In these temples of convenience
Piss smelly cathedrals
Of hush-toned obedience
And damp marbled spiral stairs
Where real men kneel
And find the answers
To their wet-knee'd, piss smelly prayers.

The effeminate is a multi-sided coin
Dodecahedron in currency
Loaded and enriched
By the many faceted importunities
Of man's hypocrisy.
He can have you sussed, stitched up in seconds
Without fists,
He's no need to slaughter
His weapon's the greatest there is …
Laughter.
It occasionally kept him safe
From the violence at school,
But be careful n'uncle
It is dangerous to assume
The effeminate a fool.

The effeminate is not degenerate
Although it has been debated
To him all reality is precious
Especially if his just happens to have been negated.
Yet this showman so often appears elated,
Hilarious,
While at the same time tiptoeing precarious
Through the fragmented, crystalline world of the introspective.
He is detective
Unravelling, cats cradling, disabling
The lies and alibis of the sub-human condition.
His position is crystal unclear
It's what gives him his unerring vision
And makes his inaccuracies
Hit bull's-eye
That's why when he shines
He illuminates the room
Making your heart beat
With more than a touch of that
Sophisticated boom boom.

Boom Boom. Boom Boom,
Boom Boom, Bang.
The aging effeminate lets his experience hang
On what he hopes is his ever youthful face
But avoiding the years is a race
Deep inside he knows even he can't win.
So be prepared for him to cheat a little
If running that particular mile, but then,
After all he's been through
Surely the effeminate's allowed
Just a little denial.
Though he may be devastated
By the onslaught of wrinkles
No amount of aging could disguise
From his eyes
The multitude of twinkles
A glittering, star bursting mosaic.
So be prepared for the effeminate
To portray and say it like it is.
He knows his crazy business
His odd agenda
It's almost a sacred knowledge
It allows the true effeminate
To transcend gender.

So remember, remember, remember
Never underestimate the effeminate child
For his eyes are wise
And wild.

Autumn

It can be all consuming
As you stand looking unassuming
At the thronging masses
As you stand
Looking, you think, just like someone else in glasses.
As time passes
With the ferocity of a hungry housewife
With the wind taken out of her January sales
And as the high winds of aging prevail
Blowing away at your pirate past
Leaving you middle-aged
Half-mast, yardarms creaking
You seem no more than a fleeting reminder
Of the more important details
Of a life seemingly lived.
You suddenly recall
All the times you could have been
More sensitive
While at the same time asking
What's a wrong for
If it cant be forgiven.

You're getting older
Years are reaching stretching
Like Virginia Creepers
Trailing around your once bonny baby blue peepers
A leafing legacy of vines
You're now more inclined to call laughter lines.
You're getting older
Something's got to give
Head's pounding a beat
You're in trouble
As a thousand thought policemen's feet
Trample down the wisdom you wore so well

For so few decades
You're almost bored
At the silent rages
The maelstroms that seem to occur
Whenever teenagers
Those indefinable paraders
Of exuberance and folly
Bully their way
Without even saying sorry
Into your slightly tarnished vision.

It's no longer rock'n'rollable
You're inconsolable, it's uncontrollable
You're getting older, head's taking a beating
Something's got to give.
The toil and troubling
Of these muddling self doubts
Leave you puzzling
Demanding to know what it's all about.
So not for the first time
You give yourself licence
To anagram silence
And it seems, not for the first time,
Life itself has stopped.

It's a cold moment
A growing old moment
These are those terrifying moments
You think you might not have given enough.

You want something to ease the stages
Of the passing ages
A pearl of wisdom
To keep you strong
Something to tell you you're not wrong
You belong

But whoever tells you
The joy of aging is wasted on the aging
Who think that youth is wasted on the young
Is an idiot –
A Pop psychologist with allusions to Wilde
But surely Oscar's greatest delusion
Was to continually give so much kudos
To nothing more than the aging child.

It can't be less than now.
Very soon, it will never be that again.
Was that distant dewdrop melancholy
Really such a rosy picture
Is what's round the corner really
Such a post-apocalyptic future.
While you're soul searching
Sinking into the quagmire of the past
Don't forget the teachings
The lessons that last
And can survive
The mutiny of middle age
Those storm at sea disruptions
And the scrutinous brutality
Of your self-effacing assumptions.
It's a massive responsibility
But one we must shoulder
Because nothing on earth
Or the seven seas
Will stop us from getting older.
You're setting sail
Not a shipwreck
Journeying to distant lands
There's a dawn on the water
Where the sun sets deeper
Making golden moments
Of the shifting sands.

Be golden like moments
Golden like leaves
It's the Autumn of life
You're holding in your hands
And do you want to crush it
Let it be powdered away
Or crash it
So you're floundering
In a shallow bay
Be a castaway grounded
On some certain unsure
Where the rocks tear and claw
At your youth once more.

Still you want something
To ease the stages
Of the passing ages
A pearl of wisdom to keep you strong
Something to tell you you're not wrong
You belong
But whoever tells you
The joy of aging is wasted on the aging
Who think that youth is wasted on the young
Is an idiot –
A Pop psychologist with allusions to Wilde
But surely Oscar's greatest delusion
Was to continually give so much kudos
To nothing more than the aging child.

The Domino Man

He was burning the games
It's as black and white as that
He was burning the games
But he held the dominos back.

He stood by the Thames
A study in loneliness
A glow from the light of his brazier
Although a roaring fire
There was no cosiness,
His past cast a shadow
This instant turned cold.
The domino caught
In a compendium of thought
Dark mysterious hazier
Than the twists and turns
Of this misguided river.
In this midsummer time
I feel November drawing
Deliver
The claw of a thousand winters
Savagely pierce our souls
Air was bitter still
As frozen butter.
Yet winds were rushing
Curling twisting
Enveloping crushing
Like a giant invisible python.
A python
Who was mourning the passing
Of his serpentine comrades
The cobras vipers adders
Stinging singeing scorched
Clinging with desperation

Onto the ever diminishing
Burning blistering
Snakes and Ladders board.

I wanted to call out
But there was no eloquence inside
Fair weather words, like friends, deserted me.
Manners told me not to raise
My conscientious objections
To interfere intellectualise or criticise
No matter the validity of my selfish intentions.
Tonight the domino man
Had the monopoly on isolation and fear.
I watched
Amused as bemused as confused
At the battered old boxes
Trying to somehow still effervesce
In that 'buy now, play me later'
Naiveté fashion.
I'm impressed
They reminded me of prostitute children
Who had worn out
Not grown old
Worn out
Forever gregarious young
In that dusty dog-eared
Dandy comic annual
Under the bed wetted never bettered
Bed time story way.

Is the domino man telling me a story?
Are the people who played these games still alive?
I'm transported to the rickety old
Junkyard monochrome
Of William Hartnell's Dr Who
Wishing I could truly travel

Back in time
And drown in the sepia tinted
Nostalgic comfortable pleasures
These games once must have brought.
This ever erratic
Past tense territory
Is a crazy paving path of
Dangerous miss matched melancholy.
He's balding, I thought.

In the tiddlywink of an eye
There went another game
I didn't get its name
Was the box red
Or was it the flame
The fire again crackled roared
And I thought I heard the game
Screaming out in pain
'You could have played me one more time
You bastard
You could have played me one more time.'

The dancing fire
Mimicking bravery
Seemed to be mocking this solemnity
Flames were leaping juggling
Like court jesters
Desperately playing at celebrity
Who could be the greatest fool
They were tireless tricksters
Tumbleweeding with Harlequin ease
Fiery formless clowns
Reborn from the embers of fun and games
This was their last chance to dance
Pirouette and prance
They were so eager to please…

Then in an instant
The flame was gone.
The flame was gone
It's as black and white as that
The flame was gone.

He was letting go
Oh no
How could he do so?
He was burning the games
Burning the games
Saying goodbye
Oh me oh my
And a great big why
I'd rather die than say goodbye.
He was burning the games
Burning the games
Alas and alack
He was burning the games
But held the dominos back.
He was burning the games
Burning the games
It's as black and white as that
It's as yin and yang as that
He was burning the games…

But he held the dominos back.

Stupid Intellectual

An intellectual literary critic once scathingly wrote
'Why does this person have to wear a dress to perform?'
I'm very surprised he couldn't work it out or know it
For if he comprehends poetry to be the deconstruction
And reconstruction of language
Then surely he must understand you can do the same with the poet.

Celebrities are Shits

Celebrities are shits
Let's face it
They are counterfeit conundrums of cantankerous conceit
Malcontent
Completely deficit
Suffering a shortfall in humanity
Incomplete
The ultimate profanity
Cheerleading with pom pom effervescence
A first prized sanitised quiz show banality
Upholding for 'guest appearance' sake
The shabby tawdry concept of charity
Thereby wilfully undermining and ignoring
Our society's needs
For a finely tuned, redistributed fiscal parity.
Water-rats
Full to the brim of their tip top hats
With conveyer belt showbiz talents
At the same time remaining profoundly
Socially and emotionally imbalanced
Powder snorting, boring, distorting fawning imbeciles
Armani suited stiletto heeled
Awkward buffoons
Marooned on Paranoid Island
Ego contagious
Prone to queeny tantrums and rages
They're only truly content when sandwiched
And seen between the pages
Of those low brow, low down, dumbed down
Damned trivia magazines
'Hello. Is there anybody there?
Hello. Is there anybody there…
Hello, is there anybody at all there?'
They're the fanzines they need

To bolster those oh so isolated egos
Responding only to yes men
Who just cant say no
They need a terrible fix
A fame hit
Let's not deny it
They're hooked up and fucked up by stardom
The yardstick they use
To measure their insubstantial freedoms
It's a barroom barometer
In which they brawl with themselves
Their own private hidey-holes
Their own secret hells.

Celebrities are shits
The glitz? The pitz
When it comes to consciousness
Oh they deface it
Glamorous flashy
Light fantastic happy
Trashy crappy idiot elitist
Cheery ladies and cheeky chappies
Who know that whilst other children starve
Wouldn't let their own little boo boos
Poo poo
In anything less than a Gucci or Prada nappy.
Larging it
Out there
Bigging it up
Always ready to party party party
Remember these seemingly radiant vacuous dinosaurs
Are only as confident as their last line of Charlie.
This monstrous misguided meteor of arrogance
Is as welcome to me as a Mammoth with flatulence
Creatively extinct, so they should be
Still trying to tickle our funny bones

With situationless comedy
What an obscene fossil
The bare bones of celebrity
Listen in the background
Can't you hear it…?
A lack-lustre laughter track
Of prehistoric hysterics
They are modern day versions
Of monolithic relics
Well past the sell by date
Before they're even started
Single minded, hard-hearted
There's an old saying in this wonderful
Business of ours
A fool and its celebrity
Are seldom parted.
Clamouring glamouring
For those oh so prestigious trophies
Oscars Baftas Grammys Tonys
The only awards
The only rewards
The only glittering prizes
That can adorn the withering souls
Of these upwardly mobile facile phoneys
As my great friend 'The Divine David' once said
'The world needs another gurning celebrity
Like it needs a whole in the head.'

Celebrities are shits
Half-baked half-wits
Hell spawn
Born again hypocrites
Whether here or Saint Moritz
Luxuriating in places
Creating trail-blazing tittle-tattle
Battle scarred by make-up and perfection

Harbingers of pretension and intolerance
They are without doubt
A truly twisted abhorrence
And none more so than when they scream from their stadiums
'We love you, and this one's for the fans'
The baying units
The idiot sheep
Who delight in holding together
This decomposing edifice
With electric lightered swaying hands
Juxtaposing their supposed intelligence
With super-imposed star-spangled prejudice
Sacrificial lambs
Splayed slaughtered
Across the altar of fame
Loving you
Because you're merely a name.
They are the persistent Judas goat
The inconsistent willing sinner
Who, if they get to kiss a celebrity's cheek,
Any two-bit C list celebrity's cheek
Then Oh Boy, are they a winner.
So how passionate can they be about their own lives
That they must hold up this obvious absurdity
As a mirror
Is it that they sometimes see themselves reflected?
Fame by refraction
Fame as distraction
Fame giving them a distorted piece of the action
Wishing it were they
With the twinkling eyes
And erstwhile smiles.
It seems to me from both sides
Celebrity is held together simply
By a complex series of denials.

Celebrities are shits
Lets face it
They are counterfeit conundrums of cantankerous conceit
Malcontent completely deficit
Suffering a shortfall in humanity
Incomplete
The ultimate profanity.

Celebrity
Whichever way you wish to look at it
Is just about
Desperation, greed and vanity.

Celebrities are shits.

Thatcherite Pig

He snorted with all the authoritative arrogance of a Thatcherite pig
Who had snuffled out and found the finest forest truffle
'Don't talk to me of creative freedom
It's about how much you earn, not what you do. Oink Oink'
I 'd said I wanted his money
To fund a theatre company
Projecting a left-field ideology
I called it an investment in a better world for everybody
A new theatrical technology
And hoped my gingham gown had communicated its message of
solidarity
That this magnificent checked pattern couldn't exist
Without the myriad of interconnected linear threads
Which weft and weave in unison so effortlessly.
I wanted him to bear witness my dress
Exclaiming courageously
Gingham to be the most socialist of fabrics.

He grunted, saliva hand-jiving around
His once rock'n'roll Cliff Richard white
Now yellowing, cracked tombstone teeth.
'Where's the return in that. Oink Oink'
What this persistently irritating wild bore
Was incessantly reiterating
Is that my world, my freedom, are not mine
That it's all about
So completely about
How much you earn,
Not what you do.
So, in retaliation
I began to whisper confidently
With a strong singsong Liverpudlian intonation
Adding, I thought, a substantial urban intention
My mantra for a solid socialist harmony

'There is unification in struggle
There is unification in struggle
There is unification in struggle
There is unification in struggle
There is unification in struggle
There is unification in struggle
There is unification in struggle
There is unification in struggle'

RESULT!

It unnerved him
That, or perhaps the subliminal power of my gingham gown
Struck a chord.
It, for a second, halted his meteoric rhetoric
Caused him to lose his piggy bank balance
For a while
Eventually he squealed
'Whee. Whee. Whee. He who shouts the loudest carries the tune.
Oink Oink'
He couldn't sing along
Wouldn't sing along.
Instead he made my music heavy,
Laboured,
Rock music of Stonehenge density
In effect sows-earing any chance
Of his money ever finding residency in my silk purse
And in his attempt to shoot me down
My ears bled
A bloodshed patchy red flag shag pile
All over his exquisitely laid parquet flooring
Bleeding, I raged at this wretched blue beast's squalling aggression
His fountains of spittle like tiny little acid drops
Splattering me ungracefully
Irregularly pockmarking my delicately applied yet firm foundation.
Raged!

Until somehow, somewhere
In my bulldozer heart
I found pity for piggy man
This overblown
Soon to be overthrown
Piggy-eyed bloated abomination
Animated only by greedy piggy ambition
Laughing at freedom.
Yes I pity the piggy man
So frightened of freedom
Hates womanpower
Yet loves Bananarama
Hates gay power
But doesn't mind paying that little bit extra
To fuck rent boys up the arse without a condom.
It's the thrill of it you see,
The kill of it
Hates black power
Yet loves laughing raucously, drunkenly
With like-minded friends at Lenny Henry
On a Saturday night.

On one hand piggy hates power
But on the other trotter piggy craves power
'Zeig Oink! Zeig Oink! Zeig Oink!'
All hail the piggy man
Rolling around in his dirty money
Pushing his piggy pen
But only in the directions favoured by his masters
Pity the piggy man
Working in the piggy bank
Rejecting creativity
Strip lit and breathing regurgitated air
A trough of halitosis he shares
With all the other greedy little piglings
Piglings piglings all in a row

Still suckling from the great swinebeast Margaret
The swollen sow of capitalism
Their tiny razor sharp incisors tearing
Avariciously at her incredibly reluctant, almost impregnable leathery
teats
Her milk the curdling sour trickle down economic lie
Seeping pus-like its way into their
Already overstuffed pot-bellied flatulent
Fat-catulent bubbling cauldron'd stomachs.

They're the piggy bank men
Working in the piggy bank
Pushing their piggy pens
Piggy bank men
Hanging in the bank balance
Garrotting creativity
Soulless pigs hanging
Their humanity slaughtered and dangling
On a butchers hook of conformity
Piglings piglings all in a row
Dressed in suits and ties
Adorned in all the trimmings of their splendid uniformity
Garrotting creativity
Signing over to their masters
Their last pigswill and testimonies
'Zeig Oink, Zeig Oink, Zeig Oink'
All hail the piggy men
Oink Oink Oink soulless pigs.

And its not ended yet
As they're still squabbling and muck-raking
Over what they seriously consider to be
Their fair share
Of the Third World Debt
All hail the piggy men
'Zeig Oink, Zeig Oink, Zeig Oink.'

Shut Up

Don't want much
Don't ask for a lot
And most of what I don't have
I'm glad I haven't got.
People say you must strive more
But this is all I want to do.
Diversify more…
But what's more diverse than me?
You?

The Queen Sucks Nazi Cock

How I adore the lush green amour of my England
No tower blocks roar, smoke does not pour
To pollute my lush green England.
I salute my England
This subtle land
Where whispering breezes go hand in hand
With foxgloves
And the gentle down of dandelion feather
The heather pinks and purples
Streams rhyme and gurgle
Hares chase and hurdle
Across her morning moist dewy fields.
The hills and valley yield tenderly her softness and nobility
I'm a million miles from cruelty
Here in my lush green England
Floating o'er moor and lake
Impervious to trouble
It seemed nothing in this genteel land
Could burst my idyllic bubble.

So you must understand my surprise
Nay, my horror, my shock
When I found out that
The Queen sucks Nazi cock.
Yes, the Queen sucks Nazi cock.
Can you believe it
That someone so royal, so perfect
Could do something so heinous?
Your Royal Heinous, Elizabeth
The bastion of majesty
Orally caressing her husbands erectile racist penis
A right royal travesty
An unequivocal tragedy of unimaginable proportions.

Does this also mean my lush green England
Is merely a series of such abhorrent distortions
Sold as a package
To an over-eager, overseas market
Who see our history as nothing more than
Rolling hills, the Rolling Stones
And rolling red carpet?

The Queen sucks Nazi cock.
When I came to terms with it
There could be no more denial.
I stand
Stranded
A million miles away
Observing this septic isle
Saddened lonely
A solitary position
As my lush green England
Dissolves into
Chaos and division
Where an Englishman's castle
Is the crumbling housing
On a drug-run council estate
Where the elderly live in fear
Relics of another age
Twisted by grief and rage
Bemused and broken
That they should be left to such a fate
In this lush green police state.

My England is a series of hells
Black bodies murdered in prison cells
A stark contrast to the green hills and fells
We're force fed as our staple diet
Gorging on national identity.
I thought we were meant to be

Free citizens of democracy
Yet we sit content
And in judgement
To single out single mothers
As society's ultimate heresy.
It seems we never stop burning witches
And this is England
My England
Where the blue-bloodied Hanoverians
Are the true blue barbarians
Who rule over this stagnation and rot
How could they not
When the head of the highest family in all the land
Our Mother Protector
Her Royal Heinous the Queen
Sucks Nazi cock.

Margaret – A Royal Love Gory

She loved being royal
She loved good food
She loved the open air
She loved being rude
Loved being a bitch
I've a sneaking suspicion
Despite her religion
She loved being fucked
In a Mustique ditch.

Loved the pomp and ceremony
Loved the jewellery
Was always elated at the carnage
Of blood sport cruelty
Loved the smell
Of the local gin brewery
Loved being an alcoholic chronic
And on the receiving end of Roddy's jism tonic
Shaken and stirred.
She loved the sound of her voice
Loved being heard
Hissing orders
'Bring me the blood of your
first born virgin daughters.'

She loved the gays
The more subservient the better
She loved them salivating
As they first met her
And watching them drown
In their own drool
She loved an adult man
Appearing like a fool.
She simply adored real fur

And adorning tiaras in her auburn hair
Oh how she loved that crowning glory.
I hope to God she loved the Wombles
Because toward the end she looked a lot like Tobermory.

She loved the horses
Loved them to pieces
Perhaps they reminded her
Of her nephews and nieces.
She loved big crowds
Funnily, not the thought of revolution
She loved being the problem
And not the solution.

She loved the concept
Of British loyalty
And swirling in a cesspit
Of her own royalty.

She hated being found out
Hated being caught
Spending taxpayers money
On that smutty resort.
Hated the Pistols
Especially that song,
Hated being criticised
Hated being wrong.
Hated the radical
Hated the common
Hated the thought
She'd ever become one.
How could someone like her
Be an ordinary spouse
So that was the end of
Group Captain Townse
She hated shellfish

Being called cockles
Yet loved human beings
Being called grockles.
There was a yawning great chasm
Between her and the world
I suppose that's why
She was always Daddy's little girl.

As we near the end of my story
Of Margaret, a Royal Love Gory,
I think more than family
Friends and lovers
Princess Tobermory loved herself
Above all others.

Whore

Part One

In the corridors of power
They drop their drawers for kings
Paramours as courtesans
Arbitrary lovers
Force fed through families
Fodder for princes
Princes munching on the royal mulch
Made of female parts
Regal milk maids
Milking it
Poor cows
Though rich.

Part Two

A hundred years of whoredom this madam
Streetwalking threadbare
The bejewelled corridors
Of her own red carpet district
Her right royal punters
Subjected to taxes of such uncivility
So she may reign down acidly
Shining down brassily
Shirley Bassily
A glorious joke
In baroque Edwardian splendour
Sadly not the last of the great big spenders.

She may also be found
Queering the pitch at her other patch
Ceremoniously parading her wares
Arrogantly staggering
And immorally soliciting the Mall
Ostentatiously looking after the family business
Or perhaps the Cenotaph
At her most insidious
Getting her Brittanias out for the lads
Dead lads
Dead lads and Dads
This vermin in ermin
Sheds snakeskin tears for
That collect inside the hollows of her crocodile shoes
Whose families she still charges unremittingly
As she rots expensively
Replacing hip after hip
In this tired old joint
Dancing decadently
On the graves of the brave soldiers
She helped sell down the swannee

Stinking of booze
And singing
Those blue-bloodied hang-dog sax-coberg blues.

So magnificent in her finery
Diamonds mined by slaves
The blood of colonised culture
Soaked in every ruby
The bold souls of workers
Trapped within the amber of her jewellery
Shimmering, glittering,
Glamorous, proud

How can such a frail old neck
Hold the weight of misery
Residing in her crown.

But for personal services
At her palatial bordellos
Oh my dear fellows
You must pay more
For a private audience
With Elizabeth Bowes Liar
The Vice Queen, ice queen, not nice Queen Mother
A woman with all the attributes of a prostitute
Without the honesty of a whore
The attributes of a prostitute
Without the dignity of a whore.

Part Three

In the gas black light of cities
They have dropped their drawers for kings
Harlots whose shenanigans
Have caused anarchy in circles
Far wider than the streets they have walked
Streets they have been
Stalked, raped and killed in
Yes, killed in
Or conveniently disappeared in
Just for making a living.

Harry, King Of Smack

Excuse one, Mister
Was wondering if you had a spare bifta
One could borrow
Honestly Mister, swear
If one sees you tomorrow
I'll put it there
Right back in your hand.
Thanks a lot sir,
Y'know you're the first person to stop for one
Er, have you a few bob for one?
No!
And thank my lucky stars you've not gobbed one, one.

It's been twenty-five years now
A silver jubilee of homelessness
Hopelessness,
No parties on these streets
No streamers or sweets
No Royal Jelly and Ice Cream
One has only the red of eyes
White of skin
And the pale blue of collapsed veins
To remind of former glories.
The stories that could be told
If only they could be recalled
Mind's very foggy now
A real pea souper
Memories lurk life a knifeless Jack
Unable to attack
Because…
Fucking Hell, pissed oneself again
Nothing looks sadder
Always happens when begging
It's the cold you see, really fucks the bladder

It's badder than bad
If Granddad were here, he'd beat me to a bloody pulp.

Yes, it started with a spliff
Never thought it would come to this
You do remember me, don't you
There one was, up there and ready
Third in line to the throne
Here one is, down and out
Sick of people shouting
'There's Harry Pot-head, the silly fucker's stoned.'

It started with a spliff
Quickly turned into a sniff of the white stuff
Never called it Charlie, for obvious reasons
Risk of treason probably,
Used to snort it in that bloody Tower
Chop it into little lines of succession
Me, my brother
One after the other
Our heads leading a procession
No mere government could organise.
This might sound perverse
After a gram or three
We were Kings of the Universe
God's riding chariots charging triumphant
Through a ticker-tape parade
Of cocaine.
Did it time and time and time again
A high higher than highness
A most exalted reign
Just couldn't get off it
Couldn't stop it
Like a royal train running out of control
Speeding off the tracks
Heading for a disaster
That would shake the throne.

Turned to heroin you see

Only thing that could calm me
Would've gone barmy in there without it
I hated getting up to all that no-good monarchy business
Forever OAP hand-shaking and baby-kissing.

Actually, to tell the truth, what really fucked it up
Was when they found the Crown Jewels had gone missing
Had to feed one's habit
When one 'cold pheasants'
It's not pleasant
You take any opportunity to stop it
Grab it any way you can
Sold them to a man for a tonne down the Piccadilly
Just before the Golden Jubilee
It was they or I
One feels one would die without a hit
I mean really die
Di?
Would've been fine if the press hadn't got hold of their so-called
Startling revelations
Fucking media, front page news
Made it sound like I was the only one
Bloody family's been getting away with it for generations.
They had to make an example,
Booted me out
Thrown on the streets to survive, weather raining or sunny
Funny thing is, begging's a lot like being Royal really
Still accepting hand-outs from tax payers money.

It was Edwardian in there
Fleur de Lis everywhere
Pyjamas ironed by silent wankers
Eyes alive with admiration
Just by being next to us

Somehow took them, they thought
Somewhere above their station
Laughing when you're not amusing
Nodding when you're talking shite
As if they were born to serve you
Conveniently forgetting their parents fight
Against poverty
Gleefully supportive of the ever cruel paradox
That part of their meagre wage
Is by some divine right
Our property.
Only now does one realise
I was nothing more than a well-hung stud
In the bluest movie
A pawn in an orgy of political pornography.

It's Dickensian out here
A wasteland of fear and progress
Super-powered execs dressed to impress
The next super-powered exec who will in turn create homes
For these career-possessed to inner city live in
Giving shelter to the given
While I am seen insubstantial
Unforgivably poor
Derisible
Sore
The big I am is a big no more
Young old bones creaking their way
To another shop doorway
Another cold pavement
The welts on my skin beg me to rest
Suppurating wounds gape in amazement
At my tenacity to cope and hope for the best.
A quid off someone who doesn't stop long enough
To see who they have helped
Or indeed how I'm dressed.

I am Crown Prince Invisible
Of the unforgivably poor
Still sore
Waiting for just enough money to become more
Or less
Enough to stop the pain

To keep sane

Only when the needle hits the vein
Does one feel royal again
It stops the pain
When the metal kisses skin
I let her in
And I begin
To feel royal again.

Further Education

Although I've never been to college or university
A lot of time on campus I have spent
In fact all my life I've been as campus Christmas.
Campus Knickers,
And campus a row of tents.

Gingham Girl

Young Chloe Poems went on a demo
For the women of Greenham Common
With some of her closest socialist pals
A rally of solidarity
Because although very much a man
She wanted to show she was also 'one of the gals'.
As they were singing songs of personal freedom
And political devotion
There came suddenly the loudest bang –
A mini nuclear explosion.
Momentarily panic overtook the still unified crowd
There were audible gasps of horror
As they held onto each other
And witnessed the nightmare shock
Of a toxic mushroom cloud.
It was a disaster of the worst kind
That held them all agog
As if from no-where there then descended
A soup-like syrupy luminescent fog.
Something lumbering green glowing
Came lunging through that mist.
In the melee young Chloe was knocked to the floor
Then bitten on the bottom by a radioactive lesbian feminist.
Immediately Chloe grabbed her head,
Was writhing in agony and pain.
Her gingham gown began to rip, tear, bulge, burst,
Really she put the Incredible Hulk to shame.
Although a physically and mentally distressing metamorphosis
It was yet another the radical agenda-bender had to undergo.
She struggled from the floor, then flew up into the air
She had become the world's first
Gingham super-hero.
Faster than an amphetamine-crazed speed queen
More powerful than the show business gay mafia

Able to outwit tall bitchy trannies with a single flounce.
Look, up in the sky
There
That gingham blur
Is it a bird?
Is it a fella?
Yes, it's Gingham Girl!
Gingham Girl, Gingham girl, flying through the glen
Gingham Girl, Gingham Girl, slept with so many men
Takes back from the rich, redistributes to the poor
She wants to give them more, make a fairer world
Good ole Gingham Girl

There are many perks to a super-hero's job
And these perks she started getting.
It was Gingham Girl who administered the vows
At Batman and Robin's gay wedding.
It was a stupendous occasion
Done only the way super-hero's can
The X-Men were the bridesmaids
Wonder Woman, the Best Man.
Batman came kitted out in a lovely white rubber suit
With the daintiest latex slip
Robin, well he came as Robin
After all, it's the Boy Wonder who wears the underpants in that
relationship.
When they'd decided to tie the knot it wasn't about just getting wed
The dynamic of that duo is kinky sado-masochistic bondage
When all is done and said.
In the Bat Cave, Blam! Splat! Kapow!
Isn't onomatopoeia reserved only for vanquishing super-foes
Often it's Robin knocking seven kinds of bat-shite out of Batman
As he's bat-roped to the bat-poles.

The reception was a mighty affair
With Gingham Girl taking the floor

She twisted the night away with Elastic Man
Had a fabulous threesome with the Fantastic Four
She got Spiderman's spider senses tingling
Rumours abound he's a swinger-
When she dragged him into a nearby closet
She found out why they really call him the Amazing Web Slinger.
Although the life and soul of any party
There was one guest who didn't thank her.
Gingham Girl's well documented problems with alcohol
Prompted her to scream at Superman
'Call yourself the man of steel, you're nothing more than a corporate
wanker'
Of course, super-fisticuffs ensued and super-insults she began to hurl
So angry, drunk and deranged she couldn't hear Batman cry
'No, no, no, no, no, no, no,
No, no, no, no, no, no – Oh Gingham Girl!'

Every Super-hero has their nemesis
And Gingham Girl was no exception
Her mortal enemy was Right-Wing,
Dark Lord of the Night, Prince of Deception.
His green-eyed ray of greed had turned normal people into
Avaricious abominations
Where there were once affordable council houses
There were now deplorable unafforable loft-style accommodations.
After many hard-core beatings and the occasional bitchy tittle-tattle
Right-Wing challenged Gingham Girl
To come face to face for a final battle.
He declared it would be a clash of titans
The fight of fights,
Gingham Girl was more concerned
There would be some people frightened
Or even worse, a clash of tights.
Right-Wing chose the location
On his instruction it would be fought in Manchester
Gingham Girl thought

'Well, if we're going to leave a trail of debris and destruction
it's probably best we do it above the Arndale Centre.'
Our plaid clad, really a lad, heroine valiantly flew there alone
But Right-Wing had cowardly brought his henchmen
Battle commenced with Gingham Girl
Being set upon by Lenny Henry and Ben Elton.
They started to do their stand-up
Thinking it would bore her to death
But they hadn't reckoned on her titanium-laced gingham earplugs
And her hurricane-force gingham super-breath.
She easily blew off Lenny Henry
After all, he's as Light Entertainment as velour
For Ben Elton she produced a quartet of talons
From her gingham gauntlet
And ripped him to pieces with her Claws Four.
Her attention then turned to Right-Wing and
My God, she was furious
By now she was even angrier than when hopelessly straight people
In an endeavour to sound trendy describe themselves as bi-curious.

Right-Wing fired his trickle-down economic atomic laser cannon
In the vain hope that she would yield.
Our Gingham caped crusader deflected it with her
Multi-layered power-to-the-people proton force field.
Now, almost exhausted, our villain used his free market forces,
Family values, twenty-eight clauses, neuron-random privatiser
But his powers were fast fading away.
Gingham Girl retaliated with a quick jab from the left
Then double-whammyed him with an all-property-is-theft,
End-the-third-world-debt, red-hot heat ray.
That blast was enough to finish off Britain's most evil entity.
Now Gingham Girl could remove his mask
And reveal to the world his secret identity.
Even while dying and lying there, she thought he still oozed sinister
When she removed his blood-drenched cowl
She could see it was none other than the Right Horrible Tory Blair

The New Labour Prime Minister –
'So, Gingham Girl, you think you've won
But this was merely a diversion for a far unholier purpose
Even now my cronies are putting into place
My plans to privatise and dismantle
Your precious National Health Service.
Ha ha ha ha ha ha ha ha ha'

It seems a Super-hero's work is never done
Especially if you're one on an emotional mission to save the world.
Look, up in the air,
There,
That Gingham blur
Is it a bird?
It's a fella.
Yes, it's Gingham Girl.

Love, Sex, Drugs, Rock'n'Roll and Honesty

Here I stand and here I see a world at war alive with hostility
Victims of political pomposity
Who's the victor? Who's the casualty?
It seems we're all walking wounded in this violent apology.
Where's the love, sex, drugs, rock'n'roll and honesty
I love, sex, drugs, rock'n'roll and honesty.

I'm somehow still standing though the rug's pulled from under me
This space in time seems an impossibility
I hope I'm not a temporal anomaly
Swirling in a vortex of man's inhumanity
For in my heart there still beats a pulse of singularity
A place of warm hard hugs, heart'n'soul and harmony
Of love, sex, drugs, rock'n'roll and honesty
I love, sex, drugs, rock'n'roll and honesty.
Self medication can be a dangerous philosophy
As I witness society administer its own lobotomy.

For me the mathematics of life don't calculate simply
Double plus duplicity equals dodgy numerology
As we're all ripped asunder in chaotic chronology.
I want to sing a ballad of value added serenity
But why do oppressed minorities
Then oppress oppressed minorities?
How can we condemn children for killing children
Without taking any responsibility?
We should be issued a warranty in this global improbability
A guarantee that sometimes we can reach synchronicity.
Why have I the temerity to harbour one-love tendency
When we've so obviously swapped
Sincerity for cynicism and treachery?
I wonder if the primordial slime knew of it's eventual legacy
That we'd evolve into a bunch of mugs legitimising hypocrisy.
Where's the love, sex, drugs, rock'n'roll and honesty

I love, sex, drugs, rock'n'roll and honesty.
We are many constellations in this glorious cosmology
We're the fractions causing action mathematical eccentricity
Capable of more than living trendily, existentially
Infinity plus one is all our eventual destiny
Infinity, infinity we've all got infinity.

Let's just take the love, sex, drugs, rock'n'roll and honesty
I love sex, drugs, rock'n'roll and honesty
Every human being could be afforded their dignity
If only every human being could afford
The love, sex, drugs, rock'n'roll and honesty.

Me

I stand sometimes noble
As I survey with dignified relish
The battlefield of my life.
I am many things in my sights
Wounded, brave, blurred, frightened,
I've lost count of the amount of times I've shit myself
As I've gone over the top.
I'm a soldier
Valiantly striving for victory
In name of queenery, not Country.
A most florid Florence Nightingale
Flagrantly singing a lament
To the brave dying boys of the massacre
I'm the last face many of them will see
The last vision of their blatant, latent effeminacy.
I am the scarred scorched remains of my tenacity
Thank God I am me.

ME
Me Me Me Me Me Me Me Meeeee
Oh Meee Meee Yeah Yeah
ME

It's a tune that wingle wangles
Around my head
A trumpeting bugle call heralding a new dawn
I've come to accept my reward
Shining medals of valour and velour
I can wear emblazoned across my chest
To prove I've lived and survived.
Survived!
Survived…
Survived?
Survived what?

My medals are suddenly ripped asunder
As I'm branded a coward.
Have I survived me?

Once again
I am crystalline fragmented
Some might say demented
Forcibly ejected
Like salt from the cellar of despair.
It's damp, warm, in there
And the air would be almost breathable
If I thought I could never be found.

I could live
Miserable, dank, rank, wretched
With only my drooling slobber
For company.
Pain is sometimes easy
Pain sometimes means relinquishing responsibility.
It's a great hovel, pity.
I could squat dormant
Howling into my own mouth
But is that me?
Where's my Dunkirk spirit?
My General with that stiff upper lip
Housing the whiskey stinking moustache
Which halos his blustering orders
Where's that poxy construct now
As I resurvey the battlefield of my life
Blind like a mole
Peering without longevity
Through the smoke and barbed wire
Of my history.

I am weary
So tired
So tired of being me
I want to go AWOL
But the only escape is me.
It feels like I'm digging a tunnel
With a teaspoon
Frantically burrowing away
And I'm gasping with joy and relief
As I reach for that last piece of earth...
Then bloody sodden hell
A new calamity
As the tunnel caves in around me
The clay and rubble
Are now my grubby experiences
Which I could no longer sustain.
I am the dirt
Under my own fingernails.
I am moribund.
I am catalepsy.
I am coma.

I am waiting for the last bus
And the last bus is me.
Ding ding!
I've got a ticket to ride
A half fare to Piccadilly
Got a date
It's my first date
Who am I meeting?
Me!
I'm nervous and perspiring
As I wonder what I'll be like
I'm trying out conversations with myself
So I've always got something to say to myself
Witty one-liners

To make me laugh jauntily
Have enough long words
Just enough to impress me
Nothing too ostentatious
Something simple like serendipity
Don't want to overdo it
Don't want me to think I'm too cocky now do I
First impressions and all that.
Ding ding!

Dong dong!
I can see me at the meeting place
Feigning confidence
At the prospect of meeting me
But I know I'm shy
Afraid of intimacy
Afraid of the deluge that is
True emotional responsibility
And although I'm pleased to see me
And find myself really rather attractive
I'm reminded by my eyes
Just how many times I have failed love
And how it's failed me…
And angry
That I can't give wholly of myself
Even to myself.
But then this is only the first date
So perhaps I'm jumping the gun
Bang Bang!
The biggest of bangs
As I impact with myself.
Where am I in all of this noiseless traffic
This speeding hesitancy
Where is me?
BANG BANG

I'm a hit 'n' run lover
Finally the accident
I always knew would happen
Broken, lame, incomplete
I should be slain
So the tribe can go on stronger without me
Don't want to hold back the warriors
The brave brave soldiers
Marching toward their final goal
The glorious victory…
But who are they
These warriors?
Who are they
Not so long ago
I thought they were me
Could they be?
Not that's silly
They could be…
No come on, pull yourself together Chloe
Wait a minute
They could be a little
Like me
The vulgarities of society are not famed
For treating everybody gracefully
They could also be nobly masking frailty
But if that's so
Then why can't they tell me?
And why do I pretend not to know
Why can't I listen to myself enough
To comfort and console me –

And if their perfect frames house
Doubt and insecurity
Has the last bus taken me to us
And does that mean
It's not just me

That perhaps
Perhaps
It may be
We.

Queers Are Niggers Too

A path less travelled
Doesn't mean it can't be trodden
A tale less told doesn't mean it can't be passed on.
Once upon a time I was told
I was this machine
That contraption
Separated
Forced to travel those ghetto roads.
My isolationary politics, still so important to me
Can also be distraction
Respectfully, sometimes perspectively
Reaching vanishing point.
So to become a different faction
I had to open out into interaction
Unification
Not talking one nation
Because I'm one of those so-called insignificant others
Some of my sisters and brothers
Of all persuasions and colours
Want to beat into extermination.
'Exterminate! Exterminate!'
This isn't the make-believe war cry of some tin pot TV alien dictators
This is the stark reality of humanity's traitors
Conscience violators
Innovators of hatred and loathing
Slavering bulldogs in human clothing
Who want me beaten, broken, dead
So it's time it was said
Queers are niggers too
We're the paki, we're the jew
But who's fighting who?

If love sees no colour
How can a virus

And I'm not too sure these days
What does and doesn't grow inside us
I'm sorry
At my most melancholy
AIDS is bigger even than division and violence
I've seen with my own eyes the futility of silence
To cope with such a raging epidemic
To our discredit in the West
It seems we're slowly pushing through
But the onslaught of this holocaust is intercontinental
Millions of lives being pushed aside
As if inconsequential
Communities swept away
Wept away
Grief raining down as tears torrential
Monsoons of emotion defying any reason
There's seemingly no end to this rainy season.
Dying isn't a gay thing
It belongs to us all
It's horrors, it's happiness
Sprawl open-ended across human experience
And this cannot be denied.
I felt I witnessed the last breath of millions
When my best friend died.
Queers are niggers too
We're the paki, we're the jew
But who's fighting who?

There are so many of us some people want dead.
We're potentially an army in minority
A sizeable multicultural majority
A supercult,
Let's not be so easily led into the self-fulfilling prophecies
Of group-induced flattery
Flattery will get us nowhere
We can have the conundrum of category stopped

Who's blacker than who?
Who's gayer than what?
Who's the jewiest jew?
Is she more or less of a woman than you?
Remember the machine doesn't work till the penny drops.
Let's undo the mechanisms of separatism
There's a wider schism to mine
Another seam that must not be left untouched
We live, we breathe
We die, we grieve
We're as alike as unalike
Vivre le difference
Freedom fighters of the world unite
We must arm ourselves against apathy and indifference.
So when we march,
When we party
Rightfully singing songs of reclamation
Resist the overwhelming temptation to believe
That self-congratulation
Is indeed emancipation
For queers are niggers too
We're the paki, we're the jew
But who's fighting who?
Who's fighting who?
Who's fighting who?

The Invisible

It's there
Tangible as rock
Vivid as the red dusk at a seaside town you've never visited.
See it without looking
Don't know what it is
Don't have to revisit it
It's there
You don't have to tell where
No need to disgrace it with words
Or definition
It's the Invisible
It's all ours
The devil in your pocket
The angel on your shoulder
Invisible lips whispering bittersweet nothings
Telling you stories that keep you awake
And longing.

The Invisible.
We all have it
The something we never should have thought
We all do it
Blink and it's gone
We feel hoodwinked
At never having experienced it.
Zoom
At the turn of a blind eye
We glimpse it.
It's the back seat driver
In a stolen car
Eyes highlighted in the rear-view mirror
Mouth half-grinning in the wing-mirror
And he's bellowing orders
None of the other poolside typists can hear

He's demanding you to go faster than your fear
Further than you've ever gone.
You stop for a second
Screech to a halt
Wondering if you'll ever obey him.
It's then you lose your rhythm
A colleague turns
Sees your spelling mistake
And your escaping eyes
Direct her to the Invisible
She can't see it
But she knows it's there
And that half-second revealing pause
Will never be forgotten
Or spoken of.

The Invisible
The outside of teaching
In other words
What we've not been taught
It can't be
Because, as we all know
There's no such thing
As invisible chalk.

The Cocktail Hour

The kings and queens of twilight
Drool the roost
In this sullied palace,
Chicken running until out of breath
And out of pocket.
But it's the chickens who are truly cocks of the walk
Strutting their stuffing
Masquerading as such pleasant little fuckers
There are duckers and divers swimming around
Drowning deep in a faded blue sea
Of crumpled fivers.
Sink or swim. Coming up for air
Squawking with delight, hiding their despair
Behind wide-open amphetamined eyes
Lost in a menagerie of imagining,
Imagining what?
That maybe one of these old queers
Will one day take them far away from here?
But they wouldn't dare leave their wives
And teenage children
To set up house
With such a post-pubescent, shambolic
Already alcoholic, incredibly inconsistent vulgar lout.
'You've just got to face it dear
The bottom line's the bottom'
They're like anglers tickling trout.

It's the Cocktail Hour
And lights are low as people's expectations.
The glimmer of hope glows dimmer here
It's perhaps a grope for a fiver.

The millionaire's in
His laughter is weighted and x-rated
With the din of excess and money
He buys us all decadence
To entertain him and this weeks dog-eared honey.
We're the hottest ticket in town
He brings out the whore in all of us
As the champagne flows down our throats
In steady streams
And we gorge gorgeously
For two whole hours.
His stories are boring
But he's not cold
He genuinely loves and understands
The Cocktail Hour

For this time every Thursday
We're his community
We feel unity in the bar when he's there
He equally distributes drink
Wants us all pissed
Twilight's rich and filthy philanthropist,
The Cocktail Hour's very own
Champagne Socialist.
It's ribald and bawdy now
As the bubbles take hold
The queens are ungraciously
Losing their crowns
But we don't care
It's party time for the brave and bold
There's a Mardi Gras in the air
The bar's alive with machine-gunning laughter
And passionate toasts to dead friends
The good time engine is up and fully
Running faster
For these priceless inebriate moments

It seems the hysterics and unity
Will never-end.

It's the Cocktail Hour
And we're burning up
On alcohol and love
The glimmer of hope
Glows brighter here
It's a party for the partied.

Mine were the solicitors and scallies
Who did more than think about men
While wanking in the mirror
Who dared to explore venture
Into the terrifying world of sexploitation.
OK, it cost them
But in a funny kind of way
It was all part of their tiny liberation
That for ten to twenty minutes
Once a month
In a stinking toilet cubicle
They could at last be themselves.
And it wasn't a slow comfortable screw against the wall
Not at all
It was much more frantic and poppers
Hot and bothered, bewildering, bewitched
A jagged lurch to ecstasy
Money exchanged
And the usual promises to keep it secret

'Sshh ..
No-one must know but us.'
This is the lust that dare not speak its name.
We were beyond shame
It's as if keeping it profane
Made it sexier

And I was a very stained glass windowpane
Through which they saw
Any number of eroticised possibilities,
An archangel using his wings
To alleviate them from their
Self-perpetuating, self-hating leaden mediocrity
Saint Chloe of the Cottage Industry
Prostitute, martyr, saintly patron
Saying her little prayer
'The only barriers to exaltation
Are the limits we put on limitation.'

It's the Cocktail Hour
And lights aglow
With honesty and lies
The glimmer of hope's
All aquiver here
It's the uncertainty of society.

Canal Street's Biggest Celebrity

I'm a Maitre D' at this dead posh pizza place
You're looking at the face of Pizza Palace
'Pizza Face', they call me on town
I fuckin' hate it
Being nice to a load of dickheads
Who don't even know my name
'Enjoy your meal sir', or rather
'Fuck off sir', you inane bastard
I'm nothing to you and never will be.
Can't wait to go out, me
Hit the town drop an 'E'
It's all there is
What else is there?
Got this fantastic new top see
It's Westwood, the business
I'm like a cat with the cream
A queen with the crown
Meow
Cost a fortune
Turn the club green with envy
Upside down
But that's me all over
Don't give a fuck about anybody
Why should I?
They're just a bunch of jealous twats
Who wouldn't know humanity
If it hit them in the face.
Well, I'm gonna hit them tonight
Slap them right down
Put them in their place
With all the grace and style of Naomi.
I forgot to mention
I'll be the centre of attention
Drippin' with more star quality than Kylie

Move over Madonna Chicconi
It's this child's destiny
Make way everybody for
Canal Street's biggest celebrity,
And it's take off time soon
So come on boys
Fly me to the moon.

I'm really off it now
Everybody's talking about me
They're saying I'm cheap and slimy
While smiling at me benignly
Pretending they're all loved up.
Don't wanna get too sweaty
Can't ruin me look
They say clothes maketh the man
But I swear they'll be the death of me.
Can't stand looking scruffy,
Don't know why I take 'E'
Makes me all disoriented and fuzzy
I feel like the most hated person in the room
But like Adeva says:
'Don't let it show on your face.'
I just look at them,
Cold and unfeeling
Even though I'm reeling with insecurity.
But it's Saturday night
That's the way it has to be
It's the way it always is.
What is it somebody said?
Don't break it if you can't fix it.
Talking shite now
But it's Saturday night
that's the way it always is
that's how it goes.
Anyway, never mind me

How's me fucking clothes?
Darling your head might be trashed
But sweetheart, you still look class.

The guy chattin' me up
Has no idea what I'm thinkin'.
Why should he? Just wants a fuck
Well, he's in luck
'Cos I'm gaggin' for a bit of trade myself.
He says he wants to come back to mine
I can't take him there
It's a council flat in a tower block
I feel ashamed.
Anyway, I share it
With this queen I can't stand.
So I tell him a little white lie. I say
'I live in a loft style apartment
But me parents are stayin'
And they don't know I'm gay.'

Takes me back to his
Do the business
Doesn't ask my name, good job
'Cos I can't remember his.
But he said he loves my top
I said 'You should,
It fucking cost enough!'
I don't tell him I get paid extra
'Cos my Sugar Daddy likes
To leave the condom off.
Don't give a fuck about HIV
Anyway, they got tablets for it now
Wouldn't bother me if I had it.
Now I know that sounds cold
But I'm telling you, girlfriend
Better dead than old.

There's a saying on town
'Only losers are alive
After thirty-five!'
I like that, makes sense
Let's face it love, on the scene
By the time you're thirty
You're fucked up and spent.
I leave the trade asleep
Haven't got far to go
'Cos quell surprise, what a shock
the silly fucker only lives
in the next tower block.

Can't wait for tonight
Goin' out in drag
Gonna be a slag-bag
And paint the town as red as my lips
Party down, shimmy me hips
With the best.
I look fantastic, bitched up and brassy
Like a real woman should
All slutty, sexy and sassy.
I'll have the straight lads droolin'
'Cos I'll be so fierce and fucking ruling.
Might even set up me own act
Mime a few songs, do some patter
Y'know a smatter of this, a bit of that
Great big tits
Shake that ass.
I really look up to drag queens
To me, they're the real stars of the gay scene
There's this fab new one,
Fanny Du Nile Queen of the Vile,
Dead funny, dead common, dead original
She's like this Egyptian prostitute drunken housewife,
But I can't stand that Chloe Poems, can you?

Too political, stupid bitch
Says nothing to me about my life.

The Man That Got Away

He asked me to believe in him, I couldn't
I could see right through him, like Perspex
He wanted to be perfect, like glass
He said 'Do you find me attractive?'
I couldn't find him at all
I said I thought him acutely intangible
He looked lost
Then in some confusion, thanked me.
He had everything money could buy
But he hadn't materialised yet,
Offered me diamonds
I offered him politics
He looked blank
Like canvas ignored by an artist
Like paper when the writers block started
The crack between the broken-hearted
Like space left by the not-so-dearly departed.

He wanted to be there for me
'Where's there?' I asked
'Why, here'
It was then I told him I couldn't see him
But that I'd wait a little while
To see if he'd appear.
He didn't like that
Stormed off
I remember thinking the cloud he left under
Was more substantial
Than he ever was,
Whoever he was
Whenever it was
'The night grows colder
Suddenly you're older'
I've not seen that man I couldn't see since.

Faith

A slowly eroding timekeeper
Stands holding in his crystal fingers
An hourglass made of water,
Moments drip, drip, drip away
As molten wax
From even the holiest church candle
A once sturdy monument to light
Now a willowy evaporating beacon of hope.
Moments like warm wax
Are first opaque
They solidify
Then dissolve
Like sugar in tea
A brief taste of something sweet perhaps
The brew lasts as long as the cup is deep
And the motives of the drinkers' intentions
For some these moments comfort for a while.

Faith is a tricky beast
It hides amongst moments
Ducks, dives like a fairground ride
Around the almosts and ifs
A shadow of something seldom seen
As whole as the space within a wedding ring.
It is the tip tip tip tapping, the rapping
Of a hungry trolls knuckles
Under a frightened child's bed
The tingling of a drug-induced high
Indefinable ecstasy
Ask the dictionary
If you don't believe me.

Experience can be an ugly ornament
Hone from the finest china

Though you may never want displayed
On your mantelpiece
Might still become invaluable one day.
It's a shame for the poor
There aren't car boot sales for experience
Such a market-place of wisdom and resourcefulness
Would make millionaires
Of us all.

I'm reminded of my mother's struggle
And my grandma's eighty-six-year-old frame
I know they were held together
By more than skin and bone.
Moments are a past-tense half forgotten
Not fully remembered.
Not fully remembering
Still means something truly tangible happened
I wish I could share with you the enormity
Of their forgotten lives.

Moments often fall to pieces
And although faith remains elusive
Experience tells me that it doesn't mean
It can't be chased around
And if lost within the most exasperating of mazes
Doesn't mean it can't be found,
Sometimes it's the thrill of the chase
That counts.

Faith is the plastic duck you miss
On the rifle range
And the prize you forfeit
For your inaccuracy
A moment that makes you angry
When you thought you were a sure-fire hit.
Have faith in anger

It's an energy that breaks chains
And is part of the immortality of humanism
An understanding of the sitting targets
We've become.

Ego is a moment
Enjoyed and endured by rock stars with guns
Who keep their trigger fingers supple
By violently shaking tambourines
Whilst blindly shooting off machismo
Targeting you in overwhelming insecurities
Because they fear the wider picture.
Ego is a discordant crystal shattering rhythm
Eternally ricocheting in darkness
It is an insubstantial echo of a moment
Becoming a very real multiple of moments
I know because I share these moments
I'm scared of these moments
Beware these moments
These are moments, moments, moments
Often mistaken for faith.

Faith is the madness wilfully misunderstood
By the status quo.
I believed you Keith, when you told me you saw angels
Believed when you tasted hell
And I'm not mad
Or so I tell myself.
Stepford Friends call you mad
When they no longer want to understand
Stepford friends benignly and kindly smile
At the pain they cause
They lack the courage to recognise
Or apologise
Because madness like truth
Is a moment they hate mirrored

In their Stepford lives.
Madness is the moment
Friends become Stepford Wives,
Hurricane building a house of cards
Whilst tight roping on two left-footed roller skates
A razor-sharp stainless steel
Stepford Knife edge of life.
Surely they know madness is a moment
We all share
I know they've been there
I know I've been there when they've been there,
Surely they know
Madness is a moment.

Faithlessness is deceit born of denial
Denial deconstructed from love
Distilled as poison
By witless warlocks and witches
Slyly masquerading as innocents
Round table sitting
Dancing full moon naked around laburnum.
To them, faith is poison
But poison is part of the life force
Held within the tree.
I'm a sap I guess
I have faith in trees
They help me breathe.
Real poison is the rejection of experience
Concocted from ego
And drawn from the venom
The spitefulness residing
In the spinelessness of man.

Faith is an understanding of moments and experience

As well as the sounds of broken promises
Crashing about the corridors of tomorrow
Broken promises
Are the wasted breath of words
That should never have been spoken.
Promises should be sung
A lung-busting trash can opera
A pitched perfect indecipherable Italian aria
Performed for the thousandth time
But always heartfelt, always meant
By gutter-heart divas
Who wear their souls on their sleeves.
Like you Lyndsay
Who understands the space between the moon
The stars and wedding rings,
Like you Brian
The blithest of spirits
Skimming the arc of infinity and beyond,
Like you Maria
Whose keen intelligence is manifest
As the sauciest Nancy
Steering her ship through the wild choppy waters of faith.
Like you Chris, my brother
Who would truly lay down his life for others.
Like you
Whose name I don't know
Like you,
Who I'm yet to meet.
Like you Michael
Whose love sometimes held me together
My spiritual glue
I rejoice in the sticky moments we shared,
Like you David
Whose conversations shone like diamonds
In a pit of anthracite
We've mined some deep and precious stones my friend.

Faith is the continual juxtapositioning of truth
It can be an imposition on the exact position
I wish to locate reality,
A contradiction in time
Or multi-layered transcendental
Paranormal elemental hogwash
A most elaborate lie.
As a poet I've toyed with so many
Conflicting themes
Even that pigs might fly.

Damn this elemental hogwash
It's detrimental to the space between my ears
It's so often distortion, the white noise
That infiltrates my discourse
The arrogance of man, we even colour sound
And how dare we suppose faith is the pound
We pop in the poor bag
To save the blind from blindness.
It's so easily the blandness
We associate to hope and charity.
Well, I have faith in my hope
To replace charity
With a massive redistribution of wealth.
I'll even admit
I have faith in the friends who've condemned me
And I most certainly have faith in myself.
Faith is the connection
Between the freedoms of the future
And the slavery of the past
A moment millions died for
A moment they fought for
Millions died so that I might
Write this moment.
Such belief in freedom
Means faith will last the mortal constraints of history.

But beyond that, faith is
Beyond that faith is
Beyond that
Faith is beyond that
Faith is beyond that
Faith is.

Are We Myra Hindley?

What abominations lie buried in the moorland of humanity
The gods and monsters of Christianity
Have more than their cross to bear.
I've yet to see with clarity
The panorama of man's sanity
But I've seen the psychic vanity
Of it's corporate use of charity
Lay waste the true meaning of care.
Bastardised, advertised, homogenised, dramatised, brutalised,
traumatised
Lies, lies, lies, lies, lies, lies, lies.
If we've fucked up where we're going
How did we ever know where we were?

Society is evil
It's terrified of freedom
It's a concept that sees them running away in fear
Into closets that it rots in
Be cossetted and rust in
Decomposing into the skeletons
It uses year after year to scare its children
It's precious children
The one commodity
Society insists it holds dear.
But if you're naughty
The bogey-man will get you
Steal away your soul
Granny green-teeth will eat you
Swallow you whole
Boil you in a cauldron,
Beat you with a pole
Until you're black and blue
Mashed up to a pulp
She'll spit, piss, shit on you

And in just one gulp
You'll be gone my child
Digested in her tummy
But none of this will happen
If you're a good boy for daddy and Mummy.
Fear and control my child, fear and control.
So, in some small way, are we Myra Hindley?

I hear she writes poetry
Has a doctorate in English
Reads, breathes, sweats
Especially when she's feverish
She's been known to watch the TV
Even use the 'phone
Plead eloquently for freedom
Cry when she's alone.
Maybe she was told
The bogey-man might get her
Steal away her soul
Granny green-teeth might eat her
Swallow her whole
Boil her in a cauldron
Beat her with a pole
Until she's black and blue
Mashed up to a pulp
Spat, pissed, shat on
Swallowed in one gulp.

But she helped murder and torture children
The ultimate taboo
The final blasphemy
An inconceivable, unforgivable alchemy
Which is a million worlds away from people
Like me and you.
Of course we're not like Myra Hindley
Society is good.

Society is good.
The homeless are housed.
The starving have more food than they can eat.
Yeah!
Society is blameless
It can hold its head up proud
There isn't a pensioner in this country needing extra heat.
Let's tickertape this utopia
Join in multi-coloured hands
Circle dance a weave of love
Across our prosperous land
For St George has slain the dragon
We shall feast hungrily on its flesh
Gorge until exhausted
Leave the carcass for the rest
The scavengers, peasants
Those not like us
Dispossessed, undeserving loathsome creatures
Of dirt and dust
That we shall turn into the monsters
Who frighten our children to sleep
It seems society needs evil
Society needs scapegoats
Society needs sheep
It can herd into idiots
Society is evil.

Society is evil
Our Christian Prime Minister continues to let
Weapons of destruction
Tear off childrens' heads
Leave them shattered, maimed, homeless
Turn to rubble their streets
Our Christian Prime Minister says he does this
For freedom, justice, peace.
Is he like Myra Hindley?

A monster from the bowels of our worst imaginings
A dark hooded creature
With gnarled taloned hands
And hideous clawed feet.
Does he breathe a noxious poison?
Is his slobber contagious infection?
Are his farts nuclear holocausts?
Does he dare cast a reflection?
Do his evil red eyes send out searing laser beams of heat,
And would you let him burn your child to death
If he said it was for freedom, justice, peace?
But who knows, if we're lucky
The bogeyman might get him
Steal away his soul
Granny green-teeth might eat him
Swallow him whole
Boil him in a cauldron,
Beat him with a pole
Until he's black and blue
Mashed up to a pulp
Spat, pissed, shat on
Swallowed in one gulp.
Power and control my child, power and control.
Lies, lies, lies, lies, lies, lies, lies.
What abominations lie buried in the moorland of humanity
The gods and monsters of Christianity
Have more, so much more,
Than their cross to bear.

I Wish You Life

It's the most inclement weather
Rain pitter pattering down
Camouflaging tears
As we mourn the sunset of yesteryear
Giving excuse for the frown
Frown made up of anger
Bitter anger denying fear
Still mourning the sunset of yesteryear
And their serious fears that let tears run
Red circles round your eyes
Making rain the most welcome
Unwelcome visitor.
You ask is this madness
And thank God for the weather's disguise.
I say Thank God for sadness.

I wish you sadness
I wish you its knowledge
It's sigh laden breathing
The way it makes the world close in
Leaving only you
Solitary
Against the world
Bleeding
Grieving

I wish you you
Even reflections which occasionally jar
That have you run ragged and pained
I wish you those glorious imperfections
Time and time and time again
Until you become accustomed to your face
Your beautiful face
No matter its age, emotion or nose size

Whatever the peculiar jaunty angle of your eyes
Whether your teeth are yours or not
Who am I to criticise
I even wish it custard pies.
I wish you your face.

If I sometimes anger you, I'm not sorry
I wish you anger, its knowledge
Its cantankerous battery ramming
And damning ability to break down who we are
Damaging of the structures of behaviour
I wish you those deconstructed moments to savour
And taste with gusto
Its unrelenting argumentative tempestuous flavour.

I wish you joy
I wish you its knowledge
The electrified high flying bewildering wonderment of
Its spine tingling ecstatic pomposity
The blinding cor blimey flash of its bombastic optimistic slapstick
generosity
I wish you its colour, scent and bouquet
The firework display of its floristry.

I wish you life
I wish you its knowledge
And the way with it all to forage
Through its spaghetti junctioning
Milky Waying projections,
The outward spiralling of experience
The nooks and crannies
Of its infinitesimal introspections
The signals to cut through its high pitched interference
And undisciplined, unhinged, unchartered directions.
I wish you a North Star, compass and map
The ingenuity, dignity of your intentions.

I wish you love
I wish you its knowledge
The heart warming grace
Of its place in the sonnets
Its powerful ability to render you speechless
When your head's full of words,
Smooth, clean, soft sandy beaches
Slushy movies
The obligatory twittering birds
The highs and lows of its dawns and dusks
Its compassionate rage
And the sticky storm brewing sweat
Of its Heathcliffe lust.

I wish you tenderness
Its knowledge
The genteel feathery down of its intricate implications
A diaphanous gossamer winged embrace from its lullaby
illuminations
A somehow kiss from the lips of a breeze
To ease you softly back into lifes complications.

Once again, I wish you life
I wish you its rap
I wish you relief from that dripping tap
The all encompassing warmth of a summers day
A way to make the bastards pay
The self satisfying wetness of bathing in applause
The openings and closings of its many doors.
I wish you the scrabble of your jumbled words
And a break from the obligatory twittering birds
The fluffy light-headedness of the clouds in the sky
The bright-lighted hedonists who don't ask why or where
And want you to wave your hands in the air like you just don't care.
I wish you to wander its corridors of mystery
Touch the empathic humanity of its continuing history.

I wish you the forgiveness that cradles the hurt
The blood on your hands from digging the dirt
And the earth-shattering climax
You so richly deserve
The slam bamming and jamming
Of its lyrical ramifications
That turn the scrabble in your head
Into the physical manifestation
That is poetry
That is truth
That is creativity
That is life
I wish you poetry
I wish you truth
I wish you life.

The Silk Weaver

I could conjure up images of gingham and ribbons
Live off the smile of Doris Day
Always setting two for dinner
And placing lamps in windows
So my weary traveller can find his way
To a home so cosy
He'll be enveloped by love every day.
My love.
He'll sit opposite, smiling content
Beckon me to his knee
And like a lap-dog excited by his masters command
I'm brought to heel
By the power of his lust
By the power of him
His arms, eyes, lips
And although I don't know why I hesitate to think it
His dick.

There is no place I would rather be
Or anyone I would rather be with
Than the man whose inner light is
Reflected on his skin,
Skin, which is a map to his mind
So I follow a route
Signposted through his pores
Travel to his thoughts
Like a gypsy
Whose crystal ball is glowing bright
With images of a rosy future.
Palms crossed silver
I jig, dance
Violin accompanied
To a place I've never been
Fear plays no part in my journey

On and on, in and in
Riding with a charger clad in amore
Or chauffeured in a pink Rolls Royce
I'm heading for the luxury
And the knowledge
That he offers me
Of a life…
So completely locked away in his head.
The charger stumbles
My Rolls Royce breaks down
Rusty padlocks fall off doors
Hit my face
But it seems, never enough to truly open him up.

I sit chilled in the Narnia of my head
Waiting for the green to make an appearance
For Aslan to roar his approval
And power me to the summer of another love.
But Aslan is a mouse who squeaked
And I'm Mr Autumnal
Whose brilliant reds are slowly fading into snowy white.

My parents offered me a dream.
They offered what they were
Together in youth and age
Happy with each others wrinkles
And greying hair.
They gave me a perfect childhood
Prepared me for the hurdles ahead
But the barriers they could jump
Didn't feature in my gymkhana
Their equestrian deliverance would never be
My winning streak.
Bets were odds on favourite
That they would die together
As they lived

Happy banal
Like the Queen and Prince Phillip etched haphazardly
On commemorative china.

Fuck Off Mum and Dad
Take your time with you.
This child of yours can't bear the pressure
Of his dead family
And won't allow memory to be the romance he desires
Although it's your heterosexual perfection
Which still fuels fires of feeling for the man opposite.
Can't shake your grip.
The third finger of mum's left hand
Offers only a noose
And give a man enough gold
He will most certainly hang himself.
Can't shake the child you moulded
Who eventually became this man
Weak and in love
For the first, second, fourth time this year.
Looking for a contentment
That's half a sixpence
And a million moons away
And unless I can ride meteors,
Crash land and cause a crater in his heart
I will never reach whatever it is I wish to feel
And shooting stars will be damp squibs
That bore children on celebratory days.

Ouch!
I'm stung by the bitterness
Of a nursery rhyme only half remembered
And empathy for Incey Wincey Spider
Becomes a choked chortle
In a throat full of phlegm I dare not spit out
Or it will hit the navel of my beloved…

Beloved … beloved.
His tongue fills my mouth
I'm happy to feel it
Like salmon swimming upstream
Reducing my speech to an inaudible moan
Slowly building to an audible groan
And to an eventual scream
Travelling again
I tread this sexual path
Pacifying the gypsy in my soul and these hours of passion
Are enough to quell the demons
Stomping around this fragile heaven
Of gingham dreams.

In the butchers buying meat
I'm shocked at the prices
Never the pain
Purchasing vegetables to accompany
Is always a treat
Helps keep me sane.
Mr Housewife suits my gait
As I trundle down the lane.
And Incey Wincey Spider
Travelled up the pipe again.

I am that spider.
My life is in a multi-coloured tube.
No way to go but ahead
I'm hoping that pinpoint of light
Is a destination worth discovering.
As I near, it looms larger
And I'm face to face with an eye
Suddenly tumbling in cascading effervescence
Mirrored patterns
Are diamond companions of a sort.
I'm being kaleidoscoped by the eye of my lover

My parents are a horse
I'm lost in thought and centrifugal force
As I enter this iris
The source of his vision
And I see me …

Wrapped in a cardigan
All woolly warm
Knitting invisible matinee jackets
For babies of pretend families.
There's a smile on my face and a sting in my tale
As I stare benignly
At frantic knitting needles
Clicking clacking a code to keep me calm
And the Valium safe from harm.
I see someone straight in a gay mans body
Want to run away
But I'm stuck to the wool of my cardigan
It's black and yellow stripes become me
In more ways than one.
What do I do?
Where do I go?
I raise eight incey wincey arms in the air
Screaming despair
And space overwhelms me
But wait!
'Spider man, spider man
does whatever a…'
I can weave silk –

Robert the Bruce spurs me on
And I'm comfortable in the damp of his cave.
Inspiring legends is something to be proud of
So I weave him a kilt of the finest silk
And hope I've got the tartan right.
But if at first you don't succeed…

Towering over New York
And thousands of people are running screaming
In true B-Movie fashion.
I'm knocking down skyscrapers in my trendy young flares
And wondering why they're scared
As I've only brought a new silk robe
For the Statue of Liberty to wear.

Held sacred in Egypt
Placed on cushions of gold
Given as a gift to Tutankhamun
As the boy king's pet
I weave him a pyramid cosy
To keep him warm in his soon-to-be tomb
Because kings are people too you know.

Feeling power rushing through me
It's like volts of independence
Generating electricity
Can't quite comprehend this new energy...
I've changed!
I like looking through my lovers' eye
Being my own spy
Double O Spider
Licensed to weave, shaking
Not scared of the things I see
Vibrant colours, wonderful sounds
Are a squashed cacophony
A new reality
And I just sit watching until it makes no sense
Even then, I have knowledge...

I know that birds what eat spiders couldn't possibly exist
Old ladies have never intentionally swallowed flies
And eight legs are wonderful
If you want to wear lots of fashionable training shoes.

Outside this eye doesn't matter.
Outside this eye is wasteland.
My job, my house, my garden,
Are the bedsit miserable of my teenage years
Almost misspent in strange translucent cities.
I'm staring at a husk
A sad, dry, knit one, pearl two, husk
Waiting to reach expansion
Longing to be renewed
And for the gift of six more legs.
Here's the gypsy again
Exchanging heather and clothes pegs
For peace of mind
And the curse of mum and dad is lifted.

The eye of my lover is soft
And gives into my weight like a waterbed
I feel tranquillity
Rocking, rolling on this gentle sea
Set adrift for as long as I live…
Delusions of immortality are timeless
And as long as I live lasts as long as I live.
I buy a song from *Spud-u-Like*
And the siren sings from the oceans throat
'Oh I do like to be beside the sea-side
Oh I do like to be beside the sea
There's not a thing besides
I would rather be beside'
Beside, beside, beside
Baa, baa, baa
The butcher offers me a joint of the finest lamb
That bleats as it bleeds
The gold in my tooth allows me an expensive drool.
I'm really rather tempted to buy this mini carcass
It will make a fine string vest for my lovers teeth
And mothers tips for a crispy coating are never far away.

A dull thud!

I look to the floor
And one of the legs I used to have
Isn't on my body anymore.
'A twinge of cosmic angst'
But never mind, you can still keep a grip with seven limbs.
Incey Wincey Spider had a wooden leg
Which Mary thought Contrary
And Polly put the kettle on
To ease people's grief.

A dull thud!

A spider with six legs is an egotistical ant
Not quite the arachnid it used to be
So its place in the rhyme is now null and void
And waterspout sweet waterspout
Just can't be called home any more
As a spider with six legs
Can appear very very insecure.

I'm a twelve year old with an erection
Can't quite grasp my manhood
In the way I would like to
Although I've been told about the man I'll become
Whether I like it or not.
The gold of my mother's ring
Continues to garrotte around my neck
The nylon of my father's socks
Offers a pungent reminder of what I could be…
Before this child can even begin to breathe
Or be in awe of his erection
And his teacher's legs spread across the desk
He is choked and stifled into a cosy pair of slippers
And the eventuality of grandchildren…

The pretend families my parents offered
Who will wear the invisible matinee jackets
I will knit.

This confusion leaves me lonely
Outside my lovers eye
And I want to get back to the visions I created
I'm banging, pounding, bouncing furiously
Off his pupil
Like a wasp on a window on an August afternoon
Beaten back by a cold pane of glass
Defeated, about to drop...
But wait, I can weave silk!
So I spin a sheet of the finest
To catch the alter ego before it falls to its doom.
Just in time
It tumbles exhausted into the safety of my web
And its final dying hum becomes the first breathe of life.
I dash to greet my tired friend, to meet it and make amends
For the humiliation it suffered in the tangles of my mind.
As I near, a sensation I fear pours into my stomach
Saliva fills my mouth
Darkness covers the spout
As this sabre-toothed spider
Venom bloated
Hurries to the kill to have his fill
And make debris of his prey.

My lover watches dispassionately as I eat myself.

And instead of feeling good
Like a full spider should
Or a hippo writhing in mud
My ears are met with

The dullest thud

As another leg joins the flood
Of the several severed limbs
Washed away in a river of blood.
I mourn the loss of something good
As eight become five
And I don't need an abacus to calculate I'm still alive
Alive, and almost kicking

A dull thud

One from five is four
Now I'm only half the spider I was before.
Polly's kettle whistling blind
May's garden is overgrown
And Incey Wincey Spider
Just Incey Win to his friends.

If I lose another leg
I'll be more me than I have been for hours
A self-confessed amputee
Bereaved of my greater powers
But you can't live life waiting for another dull thud
There's no fulfilment in that.
I'm comforted by the thought that a single house
Built in a void, will eventually become a city.
It's an optimistic fact
That makes me act on impulse.

Bang!
I'm off …
The many muscles of my four legs drive me on
Gravel sparks beneath my feet
Until I'm kicking up worms and rainbows.
I speed to my lovers' eye
And because I'm faster than it can see
Invisibility is my best camouflage.
I pass through … hurray

A dull thud

An uncertain victory?
Have I lost my legs to his pupil?
In panic I count
One. Two. Three.
Thank God I'm still not me.

Suddenly the space is glowing golden
Warm like sun on fields of corn
I'm made at peace
As serenity makes my eyelids heavy.
I know the truth of bliss
Revolving slowly I ascend.

Is this the scenic route to heaven?
I feel like a self-addressed soul
On a celestial circular
Ignoring demonic intervention.
I reach to touch the gold around me
And fingertips caress silk
A most delicate thread
Light like breath
Soft as Gabriel's kiss
And I'm being drawn to something like a hopeless man to water
And the comfort of drowning.
I twist a final turn
Lift my head
And I'm greeted by beauty.
Tears fill my eyes
And fall to form a morning dew
Droplets left shimmering like a halo
On the web surrounding me.
My lips slowly open
But communication is left to my eyes
As I acknowledge the enormity of

The Silk Weaver.

I bypass awe and fall into a frenzied trance
As the structure of oneness fulfils me
I fall to my knees, not to pray
But because I can't take the weight of this ecstasy.
What?
Polly refuses to make the tea
Mary Mary wasn't at all contrary
In fact she was the botanist who discovered silver bells
Miss Muffet was only scared because a man wrote the rhyme
And Peter Rabbit is a racist.

This communion with another mind
Leaves me courageous, enabling, empowered
And fear of the dull thud is safely tucked away.
I remove my final leg
And offer as a gift the limb which disabled me.
It is my mind, body and soul.
I look for my lover
And the ghosts of my father and mother
But wherever they lurk
I'm not there any more.
If I'm altered by default, then praise be
The fault's all mine
Because I won't sit and smile
Roast a joint
Or knit invisible matinee jackets.

Thought is sporadic and decorative
Like the Milky Way.
Age is meaningless
Once again the Silk Weaver speaks…

And I don't exist.

Gingham Footnotes

The Effeminate

Growing up in a hard working class environment as an effeminate child, was both very difficult and disturbing. The bullying and the name-calling drove me to distraction. People think that the effeminate child is a weak child, a simpering mess, but to survive the onslaught of my upbringing I was little less than an effete warrior. This poem is dedicated to the power and strength of all effeminates.

The Story of The Effeminate by Chloe Poems

Chloe Poems is Britain's first gay socialist transvestite poet and radical agenda bender. Chloe rejoices in her effeminacy and is a powerful effeminate, which is why I wrote this poem in the first place. An uncanny string of events took place once I had written this piece, focused around the death of Quentin Crisp (aged 91 – a really good innings.)

This poem was always about empowering and enabling effeminates who felt marginalised and weakened by both the patriarchal and matriarchal constraints of this society. When Quentin Crisp was due to begin his first British tour in some years at the Green Room Theatre in Manchester I was invited (as Green Room Resident Artist) to introduce Mr Crisp with the poem, *The Effeminate*. Sadly, Mr Crisp died in Manchester the night before he was due to perform. There was a great deal of shock and upset in the city, and the Green Room became a focus for people to come to express their shock and grief. We quickly organised a tribute night to replace his performance and it was an honour to perform *The Effeminate* in front of the famous Crisp hat.

This both surreal and natural state of affairs led me to being invited to Quentin Crisp's cremation, held secretly in Manchester. Alongside the artist formerly known as The Divine David I was one of only 8 people who were in attendance. One felt a strong sense of the baton of effeminacy being passed, made poignant by the effects of Quentin Crisp on my life. At school, after the first TV screening of *The Naked Civil Servant*, I went from being called 'puff', 'pansy' and 'queer' to then being known as 'Quentin', because of my effeminacy and obvious relationship to the TV character. This personal history gave the irony of the current situation I found myself in a melancholic and phoenix-like intent. Literally, I am happy to accept the baton… run…. and fly.

Autumn

When this book is published I'll be 40, in gay years that makes me about 173. Gay years are like dog years only more savage. Unlike a lot of my gay friends, I am really rather enjoying the ageing process. I'm dressing up more now than I ever did as a child. Middle age isn't the end. A lot of our gay friends, because of AIDS, haven't the luxury to whinge about getting older. Live this season of your life. Death is the end.

The Domino Man

A true story dedicated to the gentleman on the Thames whose strange ritual echoed my feelings of melancholy and loss at the time.

Thatcherite Pig

Another dedication, this time to that bastard of a bank manager way back in '85, who wouldn't fund my socialist theatrical enterprise. This one's for you baby. Moral: Never piss off a performance poet.

The Royal Quartet

I trust these poems show the depth of my hatred for these billionaire divisionalists. I hope they uncover the truth and show the Hanoverians for the base lizards that they are. It is important for me in Jubilee Year to shout it loud and proud.

Whore

Part 1 is about The Queen Mother as a Lady-in-Waiting
Part 2 was written to commemorate her 100 years of pure evil
Part 3 is dedicated to the real ladies of the night, some of whom I know, and contrary to popular belief, are strong family-oriented women.

Harry, King of Smack

As the media tells us (and we know the media is always right), having a joint will lead to heroin addiction. This poem finds Prince Harry hopelessly addicted to 'brown' and wandering the streets of Manchester for the past 25 years. The word 'bifta' is Mancunian slang for cigarette.

Gingham Girl
In my effeminate youth I would find solace in Marvel comics and other super-hero magazines, dreaming that I myself would one day don a costume and help to save the world. Be careful what you wish for.
The '*No, no, no?*' at the end of the second verse are sung to the Batman theme tune. The Arndale Centre is a monstrous 70s designed shopping mall in Manchester city centre.

Queers Are Niggers Too
This was initially a reaction to the racism on the gay scene. It then became a paean to the prejudices of all cultures, and now with the rise of the Hard Right, in Europe and the UK, I think it serves as a timely reminder about the unification of struggle.

The Invisible

The Cocktail Hour
This is an observation about my times as a rent-boy. Yes, I was genuinely a whore and quite a happy hooker. This poem takes place between the hours of 5pm and 8pm, the time I operated, a time of cheap drinks and cheap people, a fascinating vibrant time. All cities have a cocktail hour where the underbelly of a sexually oppressed society suddenly springs to life. The word 'chickens' in this instance, is gay slang referring to young rent-boys. Poppers are amyl nitrate, a substance which heightens sexual pleasure.

Canal Street's Biggest Celebrity
This is dedicated to those nasty young queens who think Posh Spice is God, Prada is everything…vicious rabid consumerists with no love or understanding of the politics of their own community.
Moral: Never piss off a performance poet.

Faith

I sometimes frustrate my socialist pals because no matter how much I try, and believe me I've tried, I can't get rid of the feeling that there is something else, other than this. I don't know what it is, nor do I have the arrogance to shape it. I would love it to be a lilting jazz tune of which I am one of many notes. I've tried to keep it as humanist as possible and it is a personal journey around my expressions of faith.

Are We Myra Hindley?

There are times when I see America as Ian Brady and Britain as his Myra. The Moors Murderers have become the Morecambe and Wise of serial killing, almost a showbiz couple. Bush and Blair. The Moors Murderers had the indecency to kill eight children, Britain and America have slaughtered millions. Bush and Blair say they're Christians. I've read the Bible and in no part of it does it say that any Christian should be responsible for the wholesale slaughter of children. I wonder how they sleep at night. Perhaps Satan sings them a lullaby. Much of the rhythm of this poem is based on schoolyard rhymes.

I Wish You Life

This poem was written for, and is dedicated to the Manchester poets I have worked and continue to work with. They are a constant source of inspiration and their honesty and humour never ceases to amaze me. This one's for you (and to poets everywhere of course).

The Silk Weaver

In my hedonist heyday I was a dedicated practitioner of drug experimentation. This poem, written ten years ago, is an exploration of those fascinating, frightening and wildly enlightening journeys. I dedicate this to the Right Reverent Kookie and to all the parishioners of the High Church of Kevins.

Adult Entertainment CD

1. The Effeminate
2. Autumn
3. The Queen Sucks Nazi Cock
4. Whore
5. Harry, King of Smack
6. London is Paranoid
7. The Queen is Satan's Robot
8. Butterflies With Titanium Steel Claws
9. Canal Street's Biggest Celebrity
10. The Cocktail Hour
11. Kinky Boy
12. I Wanna Be Fucked By Jesus
13. Are We Myra Hindley?
14. Love, Sex, Drugs, Rock 'n' Roll and Honesty

Recorded live in the Milo, Leeds, 21 May 2002

For more information on Chloe Poems, more poems, gig
information, how to get hold of Chloe's first book *Universal Rentboy*
and a whole pile of other goodies you should point yourself to
www.chloepoems.com

You can contact Chloe at chloepoems@hotmail.com

Route Subscription

Route's subscription scheme is the easiest way for readers to keep in touch with new work from the best of new writers. Subscribers receive a minimum of four books per year, which could take the form of a novel, an anthology of short stories, a novella, a poetry collection or mix and match titles. Any additional publications and future issues of the route paper will also be mailed direct to subscribers, as well as information on route events and digital projects.

Route constantly strives to promote the best in under represented voices, outside of the mainstream, and will give support to develop promising new talent. By subscribing to route, you too will be supporting these artists.

The fee is modest.

UK £15
Europe £20 (35€ approx)
Rest of World £25(US$40 approx)

Subscribe online now at www.route-online.com

To receive a postal subscription form email your details to books@route-online.com or send your details to:
route, school lane, glasshoughton, wf10 4qh, uk

Adult Entertainment is a title on the route subscription scheme.

Half a Pint of Tristram Shandy

Jo Pearson, Daithidh MacEochaidh, Peter Knaggs

ISBN 1 901927 15 6 £6.95

A three-in-one poetry collection from the best in young poets. Between the leaves of this book lies the mad boundless energy of the globe cracking-up under our very noses; it is a world which is harnessed in images of jazz, sex, drugs, aliens, abuse; in effective colloquial language and manic syntax; but the themes are always treated with gravity, unsettling candour and humour.

I Am

Michelle Scally-Clarke

ISBN 1 901927 08 3 £10 Including free CD

At thirty years old, Michelle is the same age as the mother who gave her up into care as a baby. In the quest to find her birth parents, her roots and her own identity, this book traces the journey from care, to adoption, to motherhood, to performer. Using the fragments of her own memory, her poetry and extracts from her adoption files, Michelle rebuilds the picture of 'self' that allows her to transcend adversity and move forward to become the woman she was born to be.

You can hear the beat and song of Michelle Scally-Clarke on the CD that accompanies this book and, on the inside pages, read the story that is the source of that song.

Moveable Type

Rommi Smith

ISBN 1 901927 11 3 £10 Including free CD

It is the theme of discovery that is at the heart of *Moveable Type*. Rommi Smith takes the reader on a journey through identity, language and memory, via England and America, with sharp observation, wit and wry comment en route. The insights and revelations invite us not only to look beneath the surface of the places we live in, but also ourselves. *Moveable Type* and its accompanying CD offer the reader the opportunity to listen or read, read and listen. Either way, you are witnessing a sound that is uniquely Rommi Smith.

Kilo

M Y Alam

ISBN 1-901927 09 1

Khalil Khan was a good boy. He had a certain past and an equally certain future awaited until gangsters decided to turn his world upside down. They shattered his safe family life with baseball bats but that's just the beginning. They turned good, innocent and honest Khalil into someone else: Kilo, a much more unforgiving and determined piece of work. Kilo cuts his way through the underworld of Bradford street crime, but the closer he gets to the top of that game, the stronger the pull of his original values become. When he finally begins to rub shoulders with the men who inadvertently showed him the allure of crime, the more convinced he becomes that it is sometimes necessary to bad in order to achieve good.

'M Y Alam consistently articulates the experience of dual cultural identity, of being British born with Pakistani heritage and he violently runs this through the mixer with life on the mean streets seasoned with references to hip-hop and American gangster movies.'

The Blackstuff

Val Cale

ISBN 1-901927 14 8

'The mind is like a creamy pint of Guinness…The head is the engine that drives you through the day…the fuel however lies in the blackstuff, in the darkness, in the depths of the unexplored cave which is your subconscious mind…this is the story of my journey through the blackstuff.'

The Blackstuff is a true story of a road-trip that sees Val Cale in trouble in Japan, impaled in Nepal, ripped off at a vaginal freak show in Bangkok, nearly saturated by a masturbating Himalayan bear in the most southerly town of India and culminates in a mad tramp across the world looking for the ultimate blowjob and the meaning of life.

The Blackstuff is *not* just a book. It is *not* just the opinion of an individual who feels that he has something important to say. This is a story which every last one of us can relate to, a story about the incessant battle between our internal angels and our demented demons. This is an odyssey to the liquefied centre of the brain, a magic carpet ride surfing on grass and pills, seas of booze, and the enormous strength of the human soul.

The Blackstuff takes you beyond the beach, deeper into the ocean of darkness that is the pint of stout in your head...

Weatherman
Anthony Cropper
ISBN 1-901927 16 4

Ken sits out the back, in the flatlands that surround Old Goole, and watches the weather. That's what he was doing with poor Lucy, that fateful day, sat on the roof of his house, lifting her up to the sky. Lucy's friend, Florrie, she knew what would happen.

All this is picked up by Alfie de Losinge's machine, which he had designed to control the weather. Instead, amongst the tiny atoms of cloud formations, he receives fragmentary images of events that slowly unfold to reveal a tender, and ultimately tragic, love story.

In this beautifully crafted first novel, Anthony Cropper skilfully draws a picture of life inextricably linked to the environment, the elements, and the ever changing weather.

Very Acme
Adrian Wilson
ISBN: 1 901927 12 1 £6.95

New Nomad, nappy expert, small town man and ultimately a hologram – these are the life roles of Adrian Wilson, hero and author of this book, which when he began writing it, was to become the world's first novel about two and a half streets. He figured that all you ever needed to know could be discovered within a square mile of his room, an easy claim to make by a man who's family hadn't moved an inch in nearly seven centuries.

All this changes when a new job sends him all around the world, stories of Slaughter and the Dogs and Acme Terrace give way to

Procter and Gamble and the Russian Mafia. He starts feeling nostalgic for the beginning of the book before he gets to the end.

Very Acme is two books within one, it is about small town life in the global age and trying to keep a sense of identity in a world of multi-corporations and information overload.

Like A Dog To Its Vomit
Daithidh MacEochaidh
ISBN: 1 901927 07 5 £6.95

Somewhere between the text, the intertext and the testosterone find Ron Smith, illiterate book lover, philosopher of non-thought and the head honcho's left-arm man. Watch Ron as he oversees the begging franchise on Gunnarsgate, shares a room with a mouse of the Lacota Sioux and makes love to Tracy back from the dead and still eager to get into his dungarees. There's a virgin giving birth under the stairs, putsch at the taxi rank and Kali, Goddess of Death, is calling. Only Arturo can sort it, but Arturo is travelling. In part two find out how to live in a sock and select sweets from a shop that time forgot and meet a no-holds barred state registered girlfriend. In part three, an author promises truth, but the author is dead - isn't she?

In this complex, stylish and downright dirty novel, Daithidh MacEochaidh belts through underclass underachieving, postponed-modern sacrilege and the more pungent bodily orifices.

Crazy Horse
Susan Everett
ISBN 1 901927 06 7 £6.95

Jenny Barker, like many young women, has a few problems. She is trying to get on with her life, but it isn't easy. She was once buried underneath the sand and it had stopped her growing up, plus she had killed the milkman. Her beloved horse has been stolen while the vicious *Savager* is on the loose cutting up animals in fields. She's neither doing well in college nor in love and fears she may die a virgin.

Crazy Horse is a wacky ride.